Grow Lab™

A Complete Guide to Gardening in the Classroom

GrowLab™

A Complete Guide to Gardening in the Classroom

NATIONAL Gardening ASSOCIATION

180 Flynn Avenue
Burlington, Vermont 05401
(800) 538-7476

Seventh printing, 1999.

Library of Congress Catalog Card Number: 87-90726

ISBN: 0-915873-31-1

Authors	Eve Pranis, National Gardening Association
	Jack Hale, Knox Parks Foundation
Editors	Nancy Cornell
	Cheryl Dorschner
Designer	Lyn Severance
Illustrators	Bruce Conklin
	Lyn Severance
Cover Design	Randall Leers
Project Managers	Larry Sommers
	Katherine Stahl

Many of the designations used by manufacturers and sellers to distinguish their products are claimed as trademarks. Where those designations appear in this book and the National Gardening Association is aware of a trademark claim, the designations have been printed in initial caps.

We recommend that the GrowLab be used as directed in this guide to ensure classroom safety.

As of this book's second printing, the trademark for the Grow Lab Program has been changed to GrowLab.

Special Technical Note:
This book is designed to be used with a GrowLab™ Indoor Garden. Several models of prefabricated GrowLab Indoor Gardens with aluminum frames, specially designed light fixtures, plastic trays, programmable timers, and climate control tents can be purchased from the National Gardening Association. A GrowLab can also be built from wood using the complete construction plans and materials list included in Appendix D or from PVC pipe (contact National Gardening for plans).

The electrical components, lighting design, and moisture control components of our prefabricated GrowLabs differ from the build-your-own model. Many of the references and most illustrations in this book apply to the build-your-own model. Special additional instructions for setting up, operating, and maintaining the prefabricated model are included with each unit purchased.

The general gardening information in the book is appropriate for use with both versions of the GrowLab Indoor Garden.

Published by

Contents

Preface

The National Gardening Association has been gardening with children in schools, communities, and youth group settings since 1972. We've watched children's curiosity blossom and confidence grow as they care for plants. We have listened to their questions as they puzzle out the great mysteries of growth. We have seen them renew their interest in regular school subjects that are enriched by the gardening experience.

Because not all teachers and youth leaders are lucky enough to have outdoor garden space, adequate time, or a climate that allows for year-round growing, in 1986, the National Gardening Association began to search for an exemplary school gardening program that teachers could easily use indoors, during any season, in any climate. We found such a program, developed in 1981 by the Knox Parks Foundation in Hartford, Connecticut. This program used wooden-framed fluorescent lighting units to allow children to garden in the classroom all winter.

Five years after its initiation, the Knox Parks Foundation had placed at least one growing unit in every school in Hartford. More than 130 classes were gardening indoors. The program, which now reaches more than 3,000 Hartford school children annually, has been so successful that 90 percent of the teachers who began the program are still gardening in the classroom.

The National Gardening Association adapted and expanded the Knox Parks model to develop the Grow Lab indoor gardening program for national use. We understand that busy teachers need clear and complete information. We want all teachers, green thumbs or not, to have all the information necessary to successfully integrate gardening into their classrooms. We also realize that not every teacher wishing to enrich classroom studies with a garden will have a Grow Lab. Many of you have other fluorescent light units or gardens on the windowsill. The Knox Parks Foundation and the National Gardening Association have collaborated to develop this comprehensive guide designed to be useful for every type of indoor classroom garden.

Seventy-five teachers in classrooms nationwide field-tested a draft of this book, providing extensive feedback based on their own classroom gardening experiences. As a result, from step-by-step planting instructions to tips on seed varieties; from instructions for leaving your garden over vacation to plans for a build-it-yourself model; from hints on building support for your program to innovative ideas for integrating gardening activities into your curriculum—this guide helps to ensure a thriving indoor classroom gardening program.

"I always visit my plants first thing in the morning, sometimes to water them and other times just to talk to them—it's great —like watching your own children grow up!"
—*sixth grader, Cleveland, Ohio*

To help you incorporate gardening into your curriculum, the National Gardening Association worked with teachers nationally to develop and field-test a kindergarten through eighth grade curriculum guide, *GrowLab: Activities for Growing Minds*. It will help you spark students' curiosity about plants and engage them in thinking and acting like scientists, whether you're growing plants on a windowsill or in a GrowLab Indoor Garden. We also offer a wide range of quality resources to help you use plants and gardens to help young minds grow. Because we want all classroom gardening programs to be successful, we are available as a national school garden resource. Please contact us with questions and news of your successes and challenges. We'll make every effort to bring you the products and information you ask for, and to put you in touch with local resource people.

We wish you success in your classroom gardening endeavors. We hope your indoor garden becomes the lively focal point of your "growing" classroom.

David Els
NGA President

Acknowledgements

Grow Lab – A Complete Guide to Gardening in the Classroom
is based on a school gardening program in Hartford, Connecticut, developed by the Knox Parks Foundation. Special thanks to Suzanne Gerety, and the Knox Parks Foundation Board of Directors for their involvement in this cooperative effort. We wish to thank the CIGNA Corporation in Hartford, Connecticut for its support of the Knox Parks Foundation's original indoor gardening program. It was through our shared vision that Grow Lab has become a broad-based national program.

We sincerely thank the more than seventy-five teachers in eleven cities who have worked with the National Gardening Association to field-test *Grow Lab – A Complete Guide to Gardening in the Classroom*. Their feedback has helped us to develop a comprehensive classroom gardening guide that is a valuable resource for teachers across the country.

We appreciate the members of the Cleveland School Gardening Committee who shared their thoughts and experiences during the research and writing of this book and assisted in the pilot demonstration of the Grow Lab gardening units in Cleveland, Ohio classrooms in 1986.

Our special thanks to:
The many National Gardening Association members whose dedicated gifts of time, money, and enthusiasm have been a constant inspiration.

The foundations who share our vision of a world where young people value the land and learn to become responsible caretakers of the planet. We especially wish to thank the Wallace Genetic Foundation for ongoing support and the many Cleveland foundations who helped us in the earliest days of this program's development:

    Biskind Development Corporation
    The Cleveland Foundation
    The 1525 Foundation
    The George Gund Foundation
    Premier Industrial Foundation
    The Sears Family Foundation
    The Sedgwick Fund

We also thank those corporations in the gardening industry who have contributed to the development of the Grow Lab Program in their role as NGA Corporate Associates.

For assistance with the Grow Lab design, we thank: Donald Jackson, carpentry consultant; Michael Kirick, electrical consultant; and Al Mazzeo, Supervisor, Office of Horticulture, Cleveland Public Schools.

10

Many thanks to our sharp reviewers, who spent time and sincere effort reading and commenting on the manuscript: Sarah Adams, Teacher, Starksboro, Vermont; Anne Browne, Principal, South Burlington, Vermont; Florence Cayeros, retired teacher, New York, New York; Paula Flaherty, Teacher, South Burlington, Vermont; Virginie Fowler Elbert, President, Indoor Gardening Society of America, Inc., New York, New York; Lisa Glick, Co-Director, Life Lab Science Program, Capitola, California; Mary Heins, Teacher, Starksboro, Vermont; Casey Murrow, President, The Teachers' Laboratory, Brattleboro, Vermont; Leonard Perry, Cooperative Extension Horticulturist, University of Vermont, Burlington, Vermont; Debi Eglit Tidd, Coordinator, San Francisco League of Urban Gardeners, San Francisco, California.

Introduction

A teacher who chooses to bring gardening into the classroom offers students a chance to get swept up in the excitement of discovery and accomplishment. Gardening programs encourage students to see themselves as scientists, inquirers—active participants in the learning process.

Students in a classroom gardening program witness the miracle of life cycles. They tend plants from seed to fruit and back to seed. They gain an understanding of ecosystems, food origins, and the internal dynamics of plant growth. At the same time, they learn practical, horticultural skills that last a lifetime.

The classroom garden also provides a motivating, hands-on context for teaching a wide variety of basic subject area skills—in science, math, social studies, language arts, health, and fine arts. Whatever gardening activities you choose—from conducting acid rain experiments to growing a salad feast for the whole class, from measuring and graphing root development to pollinating cucumbers—your gardening program will spark children's natural curiosity about living things, and challenge them to think critically to solve problems.

You *can* garden successfully in the classroom. Teachers from around the country confirm that you don't have to have a "green thumb" to have a thriving classroom garden. As one fifth-grade teacher explains,

> I had never been a gardener, but I decided to start a classroom garden because I felt it would be such a valuable experience for my kids. I was nervous at first because I certainly didn't have all the answers. But my students and I learn together, and I'm thrilled to say that four years later the garden is still going strong. It has become an invaluable teaching tool and is the envy of the hallway.

A prefabricated or homemade GrowLab Indoor Garden is ideal for classroom use. The GrowLab was designed specifically for school gardening. Its light configuration enables you to grow many vegetables, flowers, and herbs to maturity within a reasonable time. Its durable, easy-to-assemble frame holds enough pots for a full-size class garden. Even without a GrowLab, your class can grow crops successfully indoors. Perhaps you have a sunny windowsill or one or two fluorescent light fixtures. You can apply the information in this guide to any indoor garden situation. When recommendations

"We give life by breathing out carbon dioxide for the plants, and the plants breathe out oxygen for us. It's teamwork. It's awesome. If plants weren't around, we wouldn't be around."

—*fourth grader, Burlington, Vermont*

vary for light setups other than Grow Lab, these are clearly indicated.

If you are a beginning gardener, or are unsure just how much gardening you wish to undertake with your students, remember, it's OK to start small. A small-scale effort—a few pots and several varieties of vegetables or flowers—is a great way to launch a classroom gardening program that you can expand as you and your students develop confidence and expertise.

You may be wondering exactly what role the indoor garden will play in your classroom. Whether you use your garden as a life science laboratory, or as the thematic focus for lessons in all subject areas throughout the year, **Chapter 1,** The Garden's Role in Your Classroom, will help you plan. It offers an array of teacher-proven suggestions for integrating gardening into your curriculum, and includes many activity and experiment ideas.

Chapters 2 through 6 tell you all you'll need to know to cultivate a successful garden. Topics include setting up, choosing containers, planting, transplanting, controlling pests, and preparing your garden for a long vacation. For the teacher who wants only the basics, these chapters begin with the information necessary to successfully manage an indoor garden. For those who want extended and additional background information, we've included some sections titled "Digging Deeper." The information in these sections provides additional insights that will be useful in developing curriculum activities, lessons, and experiments.

Chapter 7, Equipment Care and Maintenance, provides clear information to help you address electrical problems and properly care for your equipment.

Chapter 8, Sharing the Excitement and Building Support, describes ways to build on the natural enthusiasm that an indoor school gardening program generates, both in school and in the community. This chapter describes ways to include parents, other teachers, administrators, and community members in your program. It also suggests ways to encourage the media to highlight your program, and explains how to approach local organizations and individuals for donations of technical assistance and supplies.

The Appendices offer a wide range of useful information, including a comprehensive indoor gardening Growers' Guide, which may well become your favorite section. It contains charts with specific growing information on every recommended vegetable, flower, and herb, as well as detailed planting and harvesting instructions. The appendices include complete plans for building your own Grow Lab, information on purchasing supplies, reproducible worksheets, and an annotated reference section, which lists books, audiovisual materials, organizational resources, and suppliers of gardening equipment and seeds.

We suggest that you read through the Contents to understand the breadth of information included in the guide. The guide is organized so that it can be an efficient reference. If you are new to gardening indoors, you should read the entire book and study Chapters 1 through 6 before embarking on your gardening project.

"The first time I ever heard from some parents was when they began calling to find out about the indoor garden that their children were describing at home."
— *third-grade teacher, Hartford, Connecticut*

Below is a key to the symbols you'll find in the text:

Additional background information. These sections will help you develop lessons and activity ideas in addition to those described in Chapter I.

Highlights of indoor garden activities developed in classroom field-test sites across the country.

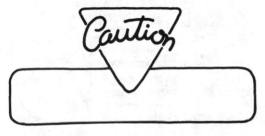

Important safety information.

note:

Helpful additional information. These notes sometimes highlight differences between the pre-fabricated and build-your-own GrowLabs.

"My principal had never visited my classroom in all the time I had worked at the school. When I set up the garden, he became so intrigued with the whole concept that I offered him a pot, some soil, and a few seeds of his own. Now he comes in almost every day to check on his cucumbers and see what my students are up to."

—fifth-grade teacher, Hartford, Connecticut

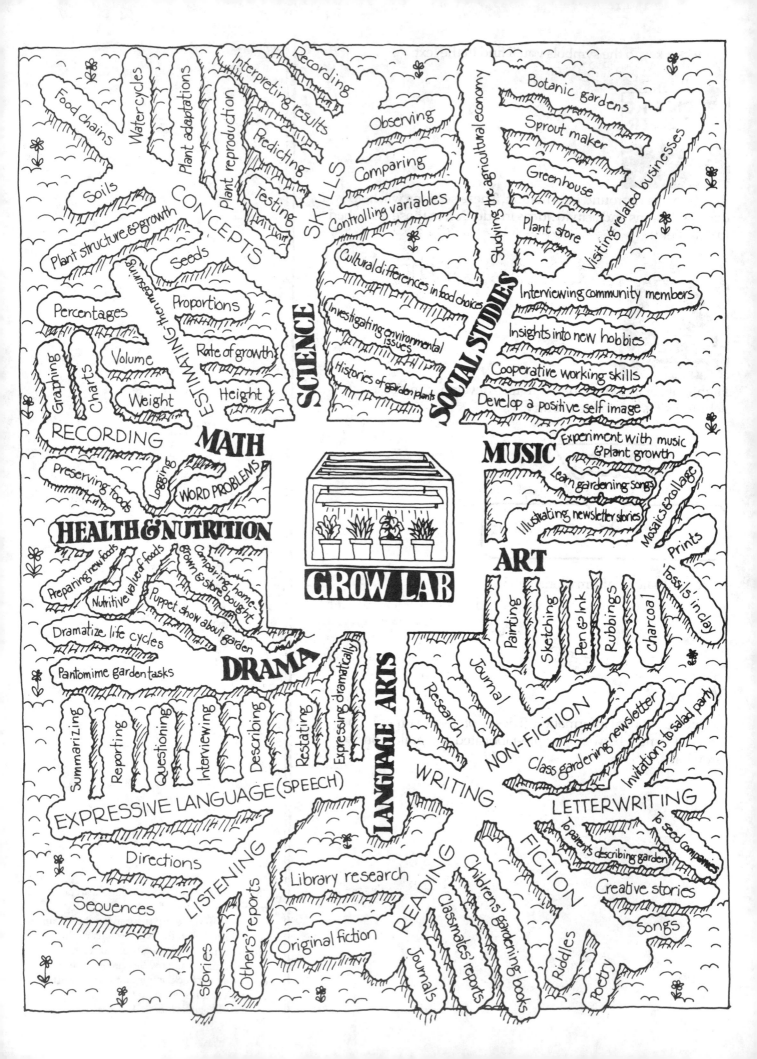

Chapter 1

The Garden's Role in Your Classroom

Just as any gardener needs to consider personal growing preferences in deciding how to manage a garden plot, so each teacher has to decide how indoor gardening best fits his or her own teaching style. Some teachers like to use the garden once a year as an exciting addition to the regular science, math, social studies, or language arts program. Others use the indoor garden as a thematic centerpiece for a year-long interdisciplinary curriculum. The drawing on the previous page is a visual representation of an interdisciplinary approach to classroom gardening.

This chapter offers many ideas for using the garden to enrich your curriculum in all subject areas. It also describes several exciting ongoing classroom garden projects which provide a culminating activity for the class. Your garden can play several roles at the same time. For example, the salad garden can also serve as a laboratory for plant science experiments. While raising plants for holiday gifts, students can also study the water cycle, measure and chart plant growth rates, keep garden journals, research the histories of different foods, write "garden mysteries," and more!

Science Activities

The process of science is not limited to any one fixed method or approach. Science is a dynamic, multi-faceted endeavor. We all use scientific process skills as we explore the world around us. This includes observing, classifying, inferring, measuring, predicting, organizing and interpreting data, forming hypotheses, and identifying variables.

The indoor garden provides an exciting opportunity to learn and practice these science process skills. We recommend using the following Garden Experiments For Growing Minds sequence to guide controlled classroom experiments. It uses garden metaphors in place of traditional scientific method steps.

Garden Experiments for Growing Minds

1. **Plant a question.** Children are naturally curious about their environment. Their imaginative musings and questions can become the basis for scientific investigations. As students observe and explore their indoor garden, encourage constant questions. Help students identify questions that can lead to a garden experiment.

2. **Sprout a guess.** Encourage students to make educated guesses to answer their questions, predicting the outcome of their experiment.

3. **Design a growing experiment.** Decide together which crops you'll use and how you'll set up your experiment. When planning experiments that include growing plants, it's often best to choose quick-maturing crops such as radishes or lettuce. Experiments with these crops can be done almost any time, while experiments with slower-growing crops like tomatoes need to be started early. Beans are a good crop to use for studying full life cycles. Corn is a good crop to use for measuring growth rates in response to different variables, but it's too tall to be grown to maturity under lights.

   Use your Growers' Guide (Appendix A) to determine planting times, so important steps in the experiment won't coincide with a school vacation.

   Control variables. Arranging for all but the experimental varible to remain constant is an important part of any scientific experiment. In the classroom garden you can keep heat and light relatively constant. If you are keeping light constant, be sure to rotate plants occasionally to ensure equal treatment. (See page 44 for more on light.) There will also be differences in temperature and humidity between the edges of the GrowLab and the middle. Water and fertilizer are other variables you and your students can control.

   To ensure a big enough sample for drawing conclusions, plant at least two containers of each type of seed or plant for each treatment. This repetition will increase confidence in your experimental conclusions.

4. **Record fruitful observations.** Observing and recording data are both essential parts of the scientific process and important gardening practices. Below is a list of the types of observations you and your students can make during experiments:

Thinking Like a Scientist

CLASSROOM PROFILE

Students in one fifth-grade classroom were curious about the effectiveness of different growing mixes, so they set up this experiment.

1. **Plant a question:** Do tomatoes produce more fruit when the plants are grown in sand, clay, soilless mix, or garden soil?

2. **Sprout a guess:** From what we've learned about soils, we believe that the plants will grow best in the rich garden soil. We're not sure whether the sand or soilless mix will support better growth. Because they are both so light and well drained, we believe that plants will grow equally well in sand and soilless mix. Since clay is so heavy and poorly drained, we predict that the seedlings will grow poorly in it because they will have poor root growth and less oxygen available.

3. **Design a growing experiment:** We will fill two 6-inch pots with each of the four growing media. We will plant two three-week-old tomato seedlings in each of the eight pots.
   Control variables. In order to control the variables, we will put all of the pots in the center of the GrowLab and we'll water each pot with 1 cup of water twice a week. (We won't fertilize any of the plants since we assume that the four mixes have different nutrients available and we want to see how that affects the growth of the plants.)

4. **Record fruitful observations:** We will measure and chart the height of the seedlings every day, taking an average of the height of the seedlings in each pot. We will observe the color of the leaves, number of leaves, and, eventually, the number of flowers and weight of fruit. When the plants have matured, we will pull them up and examine their root systems, making an estimate of total root length. We will record our observations.

5. **Harvest conclusions:** We will use the records of our observations to describe how the tomato plants grew in each of the four growing mixes. We will base our final conclusion on the total weight of fruit produced in each pot.

Measure and weigh the plants (fruit, foliage, roots) at predetermined intervals or at the end of the experiment. Graph the results.

Measure and count fruits and flowers.

Describe, compare, and contrast the appearance of plant parts as seen with and without a microscope.

Describe, compare, and contrast the taste of edible plant parts and fruits.

Describe observations with narratives, graphs, charts, drawings, and photographs.

5. **Harvest conclusions.** Students can summarize results and draw conclusions in written and/or oral form. If conclusions contradict conventional scientific wisdom (e.g., students find that plants grow better in the dark than in the light!), have students generate ideas to explain why they might have gotten their unusual results.

Once students have drawn conclusions, they can apply new information to other situations and make fresh predictions. Your science experiments will hopefully stimulate more questions and lead to further investigations, and the cycle will begin again. So, plant a question and watch it grow!

Below you'll find a few ideas for plant, physical, and earth science activities in the classroom garden. Those marked with ✱ are appropriate for controlled classroom experiments.

Plant Science

What are the differences between living and nonliving things? How are humans like plants? How are they different? Distinguish and describe differences and similarities.

What are the similarities and differences among seeds? Sort and classify seeds according to their characteristics.

How do seeds work? Observe and identify the functions of seed parts.

✱ Do vegetable seeds germinate better in light or dark? (At what depth do they germinate most quickly? At what temperature do they germinate most quickly?)

How does a plant grow? Investigate the functions of different plant structures (cotyledons, roots, stems, leaves, flowers, fruits).

What do plants need to grow? Do all plants need the same things? Study the various conditions that different plants need to grow.

✱ How does crowding affect the growth and quality of plants?

Will vegetable plants grow differently in clay, sand, and garden soil?

How do roots grow? Plant a seed against the side of a clear glass or plastic container and observe root growth.

✱ Will plants grow faster if they are fed every day?

✱ Do plants really grow in the direction of light?

✱ Do shoots always grow up and roots always grow down?

✱ What would happen if we watered our plants with tea, soft drinks, etc.?

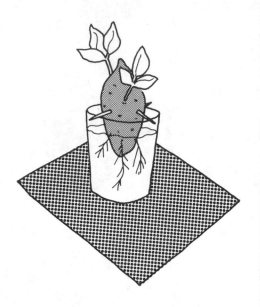

How do plants reproduce? Dissect flowers. Pollinate cucumbers. Start plants from cuttings, bulbs, tubers, spores.

How do plants use energy from the sun to make food?

* Do plants need light to photosynthesize? Try using black paper to block the light from some leaves for a period of time. Use iodine to test whether the lack of light prevents starch production.

* Could plants live without CO_2 entering through the leaves? Cover some of the leaves on some plants with petroleum jelly to test this question.

What is the life cycle of a flowering plant? Observe and record the stages of the life cycle from seed to fruit to seed.

* How can we get our tomatoes to ripen earlier?

* Do plants respond to different durations of light? Use your timer to investigate this.

Earth Science

What is a water cycle? How does it work? Simulate the water cycle in the indoor garden by covering it with a "dome" of clear plastic. Study and observe the transpiration, evaporation, and condensation of water.

How are some soils different from others? Compare and contrast the properties of different types of soils (density, air spaces, living organisms, composition, texture, smell, appearance).

How do different plants respond to different climates? Create different climates in your indoor garden and observe plant growth.

* How might acid rain affect the growth of plants? Water plants with solutions of different pH and observe differences in plant growth.

Physical Science

* What is pH? How does it affect plants? Use litmus paper or test kits to test the pH of different soils. Investigate how plants respond to soils with different pH levels.

* What are the properties of different types of light? Cover pots with cellophane of different colors to screen out all but one wavelength of light from plants. Observe plant growth.

How does energy change to matter during photosynthesis?

How does water change from a liquid to a gas state in the indoor garden?

Environmental Science

Investigate food chains and webs.

Simulate soil erosion in your classroom garden. Observe the difference in soil loss when water is splashed on a tilted planted pot, and on a tilted unplanted pot.

Compare and contrast outside ecosystems with your indoor garden ecosystem. How are they similar and how are they different?

✱ Conduct an experiment to simulate the effects of road salt on plant growth. Water plants with salt solutions of various strengths and observe differences in plant growth.

Research the accumulation of harmful substances in the food chain.

Discuss the concept of seed diversity. Try saving some of your own seeds to plant again.

Observe and compare wild plants and cultivated plants.

Incorporating Other Subjects

In addition to its role as a science laboratory, your classroom garden can act as a springboard for lessons in math, social studies, language arts, health and nutrition, and music, drama, and art. The lists that follow represent just a sampling of subject area activities with a gardening focus. The possibilities are endless!

Math

Calculate the number of hours that the timer should be on and off. How many hours a week or month will it be on?

Measure and graph the growth rates of plants and make predictions regarding future growth. Use metric measurements.

Keep records of size comparisons and use bar graphs to illustrate.

Predict dates of germination and maturity based on information from seed catalogs.

Plan backwards from salad party or other harvest date to determine when each crop should be planted.

Estimate the number of 6-inch pots that could fit into your indoor garden.

Measure part of a root and estimate the length of the entire root system on a plant. Lay pieces end to end and measure.

Use graph paper to make a map to scale of the area of your garden.

Calculate amounts of fertilizer to use per quart and per liter of water.

Chart temperatures of the air and soil in your garden in Fahrenheit and centigrade.

Determine the weight and volume of soil mix when wet and dry.

Compare prices of produce in markets to determine the value of your garden produce.

Count the total number of flower buds, and the number of buds that actually produce fruit. Figure a percentage or fraction of the total that fruited.

Project the amount of profit that can be made from a plant sale and plan accordingly.

Social Studies

Research and report on cultural/ethnic differences in food consumption and gardening practices.

To enhance a study of economic crops, try growing cotton, corn, soybeans, or wheat. (Most cannot be grown to maturity indoors.)

Research local agricultural history.

Interview local gardeners and find out what makes them choose to garden (pleasure, economics, health, etc.).

Visit some local farms and interview farmers about choice of crops, growing practices, marketing, and farm history.

Collect clippings and discuss how advertising influences our food choices.

Study the contribution of native American and other cultures' foods to our history and diet.

Research the histories of classroom garden plants. Discover where they originated, the impact they've had on our diets, and how today's varieties differ from the original plants.

Study some of the political, ecological, and economic reasons for hunger and what can be done locally and globally to eradicate it.

Use the classroom garden to complement a study of the influence of climate on food production.

Language Arts and Reading

Make written observations of daily changes in your garden plants.

Write, illustrate, and publish a collection of garden stories and poems.

After careful observation, brainstorm for adjectives to describe each plant in your garden.

Study new vocabulary that relates to plants and gardens.

Write letters to local merchants explaining your gardening project and asking for donations of supplies.

Write a list of questions about the garden that the class would like to answer through library research.

Write a letter to parents describing the indoor garden.

Publish a class newsletter about the garden and distribute it to other classrooms.

Read daily newspapers and magazines and bring in articles that relate to gardening, agriculture, hunger, nutrition, etc.

Write letters to the local county Cooperative Extension Service or garden club to ask advice and invite guest speakers.

Write creative stories in the first person from the point of view of a particular plant in the indoor garden.

Use the library to research information about particular plants. Where did they originate? How are they used? Do they require special care? When will they be ready for harvest? Prepare a written or oral report.

Put together a class book with gardening information and advice.

Learn to use seed catalogs.

Cotton, Deserts, Rain Forests

CLASSROOM PROFILE

One third-grade teacher complemented part of his social studies curriculum by growing cotton in a Grow Lab. With some skepticism, his class planted the seeds to enhance a unit on Black history. Nine months later, much to the surprise and delight of the students and teacher, they harvested thirty cotton bolls from four plants. The students have saved the seeds and next year they plan to try cleaning and spinning some of their harvest!

The same teacher incorporated his Grow Lab into a study of climates. Since this class had *two* indoor gardens, students were able to simulate a desert climate in one and a tropical climate in the other. The desert climate Grow Lab was kept very dry and housed cacti and other desert-type plants. The tropical Grow Lab housed many houseplants of tropical origin. It was kept enclosed in a plastic tent, the base material was kept constantly moist, and plants were misted twice a week.

The students speculated about how plants would grow in their respective suitable climates and made careful observations. As a final project, the students developed some questions (e.g., What would happen if we tried to grow cactus in a tropical climate?). They hypothesized about likely results and then observed and recorded what actually happened when they tried it.

Write a script and produce a play or puppet show about plants and gardens.

Choose one of the children's books from the resource section (Appendix E) to read and discuss with the class.

Choose your favorite garden vegetable. List its strong points, then write a script for a sixty-second advertisement designed to get more people to grow and eat it!

Health and Nutrition

Compare the importance of nutrients in the health of humans and of plants.

Study the nutritive value of the various crops in your garden.

Determine from which parts of the plants various foods come. Discuss the difference in nutritional value of various plant parts.

Study adaptations of plant parts that make them good food sources.

Sprout various seeds for eating.

Prepare vegetables in exciting new ways.

Conduct a blindfolded taste test using classroom vegetables and supermarket vegetables.

Experiment with food preservation techniques such as drying, freezing, and canning.

Art, Music, and Drama

Create paintings and drawings of garden plants.

Paint a class garden mural to hang in the hallway.

Design labels to mark pots and flats.

Make a seed mosaic collage.

Make prints from various plant parts.

Design a food or garden collage.

Make puppets and present a play about garden life, ecosystems, food concerns, etc.

Dramatize the life cycles of garden vegetables.

Pantomime various gardening tasks (transplanting, fertilizing, sowing seeds, pollinating).

Learn a collection of songs that relate to food, gardens, and the environment. ("The Garden Song," by Dave Mallett, is a fun song for all ages. NGA's *Guide to Kids' Gardening*, listed in the resource section, contains the words and music for this song.)

Listen to the music of composers inspired by nature.

Experiment with the effects of music on plant growth, health, and behavior.

Design invitations and a menu for your salad party.

Design flyers for a seedling or potted plant sale.

Build clay or tissue paper models of flowers.

Make plant fossils in clay.

Using a movie camera with single-frame capability, make a time-lapse film of a plant growing.

The annotated resource section describes reference books which, along with your own textbooks, will help you expand your activity ideas.

Ongoing Classroom Garden Projects

Many teachers choose to design an ongoing classroom garden project that culminates with a special event (i.e. salad party, seedling sale, etc.). An ongoing project can also incorporate many of the activities and experiments listed on the previous pages.

The Food Garden

You can grow vegetables, herbs, and fruits to be harvested and tasted throughout the year, or you can time the planting of your crops to produce a single harvest feast. Producing a tasty garden salad for the whole class is a popular culminating activity that generates excitement and group pride in a job well done. In planning a garden for a particular harvest date, you'll need to plant crops at different times, since crops differ in the number of days it takes to reach maturity. To calculate when to plant each crop, have your children consult the Growers' Guide (Appendix A) for information on days to maturity and count back from the desired date of harvest. The Growers' Guide includes yield and harvest information for each vegetable.

Table 1 provides a sample schedule for a salad garden for a class of thirty assuming that you're aiming for a May 15-June 1 harvest date.

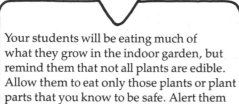

Your students will be eating much of what they grow in the indoor garden, but remind them that not all plants are edible. Allow them to eat only those plants or plant parts that you know to be safe. Alert them to the dangers of eating other plant material.

Salad Garden Planning Guide			Table 1
	Planting Date	# 6-Inch Pots	Plants Per Pot
Tomatoes	February 15	2-4	1
Basil	March 15	1	4
Parsley	March 15	1	2-3
Lettuce	March 15	8	4
Beans	March 15	1	2
Carrots	March 15	2	6
Beets (for greens)	March 15	2	3
Cucumbers	March 15	1	1
Radishes	April 10	3	4-6
Sprouts	May 10	(see below)	

If plants go home during freezing weather, you must protect them. A paper bag folded and stapled shut usually provides good protection. A leakproof plastic bag inflated and sealed with a knot or a twist tie also works well.

The Gift Plant Garden

Many gardening teachers like to have each child grow a pot of flowers, herbs, vegetables, or a houseplant to take home, often for holidays. Flowers for Mother's Day are always a big hit. Zinnias and marigolds are popular flowers for this purpose.

When choosing plants to grow and send home, consult the Growers' Guide (Appendix A) and/or seed packets to determine how far in advance you should plant the seeds. Give the plants an extra week or two of growing time to make sure they each have at least one blossom when it's time to send them home.

You can grow gift plants in small containers such as school milk cartons (make a drainage hole in each container with a sharp pencil). Plants will need to be transplanted into larger containers when they get home.

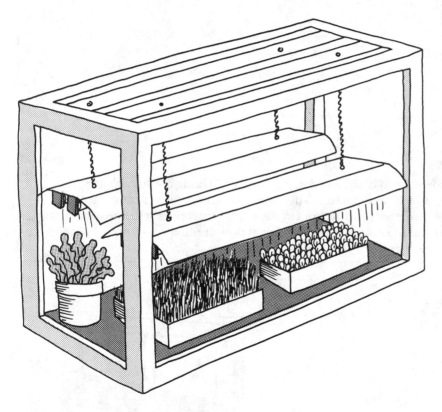

The Seedling Garden

The indoor garden is perfect for starting vegetables, herbs, or flowers, that will eventually find their way into a garden or landscape at home or at school. Classes have raised seedlings indoors for many uses including:

> school beautification (planting around flagpole, borders or around trees)
> class or school gardens
> community or food bank gardens
> nursing home gardens
> seedling sales

Seedlings are commonly started in milk cartons or in more traditional seed starting containers, such as plastic market packs. Have your students consult garden books, seed catalogs, seed packets,

DIGGING DEEPER

Topping It Off With Sprouts

Sprouting seeds to top off your garden salad can be a tasty as well as an educational experience. Sprouting seeds enhances their nutritional value by increasing the amount of protein, minerals, and vitamins they provide.

Some questions for investigation during the sprouting activity might include the following: What is a sprout? What do the seeds need to sprout? Can we identify different parts of the plant in a sprout? Why are they so nutritious? When do they turn green?

Although you can sprout many types of seeds for eating, it's best to start with mung bean or alfalfa seeds. (Other seeds that may be sprouted for eating include buckwheat, kidney beans, radishes, and clover.) Buy seeds that have been specifically designated for sprouting to ensure that they have not been treated with fungicides. (These untreated seeds are available in health food stores, in some supermarkets, and through many seed catalogs.)

To Sprout Seeds:

1. Soak 2 tablespoons of alfalfa seeds or 5 tablespoons of mung bean seeds overnight in water. Drain and place seeds in a quart jar. Cover the jar with cheesecloth, secured with a rubber band.

2. Place the jar on its side (or tipped slightly downward for better drainage) in a warm (not hot), dim or dark place. Twice a day, rinse seeds with cool tap water and make sure to drain them well through the cheesecloth before replacing the jar on its side.

3. After several days, place the jar in the light for a day or two to encourage green color (as photosynthesis begins) and vitamin production.

4. Enjoy them with your salad!

and local resources (nurseries and the county Cooperative Extension Service, for example) to determine the best times to transplant specific crops outdoors in your area. This will help you plan your indoor planting schedule. Determine your area's last spring frost date. Then have children count back the number of weeks indicated for each crop and start your seeds accordingly.

Not all crops transplant well. Many crops, such as peas and squash, have tender root systems and may be shocked from transplanting. Others, such as root crops, develop small, misshapen, hairy roots if transplanted. Table 3 shows which crops are suitable for transplanting.

Seedling Garden Planning Guide — Table 3

Crop	Number of Weeks from Seeding to Transplanting Outdoors
Broccoli	5-7 weeks
Cauliflower	5-7
Cabbage	5-7
Celery	10-12
Cucumbers*	3-4
Eggplant	6-8
Leeks	8-10
Lettuce	3-6
Melons*	3-4
Onions	6-8
Parsley	6-8
Peppers	6-8
Tomatoes	6-8

All annual flowers and herbs listed in the Growers' Guide are suitable for transplanting. Check seed packets to determine when to sow and transplant.
*These crops have very sensitive root systems that react poorly to transplanting. To avoid transplant shock, start them in peat pots or other containers that can be planted directly into the ground.

DIGGING DEEPER

Hardening Off Seedlings

If you've raised seedlings to be transplanted outside, you'll need to help them become accustomed to outdoor conditions so they'll survive the change in environments. This is called hardening off. The best way to harden off plants is to place them outdoors in a cold frame — an unheated enclosure with a removable cover. You can make a temporary cold frame by placing a storm window or door over hay bales arranged to form walls. During the day, raise or remove the cover completely, as long as temperatures stay above freezing. Replace the cover at night. After about two weeks, the seedlings can safely be exposed to the outdoors and planted. If you have neither the space nor the materials for a cold frame, you can harden off seedlings by placing them outside in a partially sheltered spot for progressively longer periods each day, bringing them indoors at night.

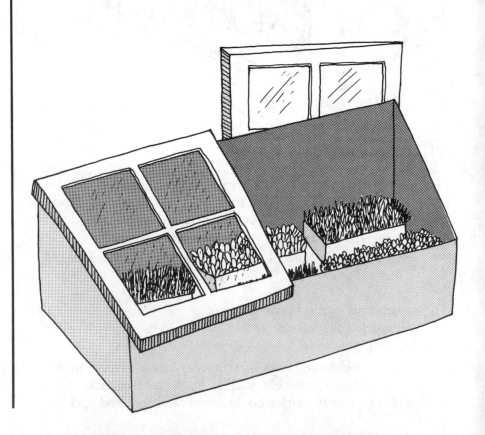

Classroom Gardening and Social Skills

Gardening provides a unique opportunity for promoting personal growth and for demonstrating the value of responsibility, cooperation, and group problem solving.

One fifth-grade teacher reported that several of her tough, apathetic students became exuberant, responsible caretakers of their precious plants. Others have noted that withdrawn or disabled students have become intrigued with the classroom garden and felt proud of their accomplishment as their plants thrived. In most cases, children develop respect for the class effort and for the living things which they've so carefully tended.

Collaboration and Teamwork

In a seventh-grade classroom, students wondered, "How do various soils affect the growth of lettuce?" The class developed hypotheses, then divided into groups. Each group tested one hypothesis. They later collaborated on developing conclusions. Then the students discussed how the contribution of each individual had strengthened the cooperative efforts of the whole class, and they noted the value of collaboration in solving complex problems.

One approach to organizing an indoor gardening project is to set up "Expert Teams" — small groups of children who become responsible for a particular aspect of gardening, i.e., fertilizer, light, water, heat and humidity. Each team researches its particular area and becomes the resource for the rest of the class on that topic.

Teachers often wonder whether it's best to have each child take responsibility for planting and caring for one pot, or to have a more communal project, with everyone working to care for all of the plants and sharing in the final harvest party or plant sale.

Communal planting and caretaking may reduce the likelihood that one child will be greatly disappointed by a crop failure in one pot. On the other hand, the potential for a boost in individual pride and self-confidence as students care for their own plants is so great, that you may choose to take that risk. Most teachers find that it makes sense to combine both approaches during the year. In any case, try to make sure there are a few healthy replacement plants available.

In general, the more you involve the children in *all* aspects of the gardening process — setting up the garden, designing and implementing experiments, questioning and initiating investigations — the greater the potential for positive social growth.

CLASSROOM PROFILE

Fundraising With Seedlings

Some classes use their gardening skills for entrepreneurial ventures. One ambitious sixth-grade gardening classroom decided to raise enough seedlings and houseplant cuttings to help finance a class trip. Students planned and projected income based on the fact that their single 8-square-foot Grow Lab could hold over 100 school milk cartons, or three dozen 5-by-7-inch market packs.

In the fall, students started houseplant cuttings, marigolds, and herbs for gift plants, and sold them at a holiday plant sale. After winter vacation, they started garden seeds for a spring seedling sale.

As a part of this project, the students studied seed catalogs and other references, then wrote and designed information sheets to go with each plant. They had the opportunity to project income, plan and handle the sales, offer advice to others, and learn some valuable gardening skills. The added bonus of the $200 income helped finance an exciting class field trip from New Jersey to Washington, D.C.

Chapter 2

Setting Up Your Indoor Garden

No matter what kind of indoor garden you're using, you'll need to decide on the best location in your room and what kind of base material and covering to use. You'll need to decide what kind of growing mix, containers, and fluorescent light tubes to buy, and how to set up your fixtures or organize a small windowsill garden.

Be sure to discuss the location and other aspects of your gardening project ahead of time with the school custodian. Explain the program and the operation of the equipment. Ask the custodian's advice about where to place your classroom garden so that it will not be an inconvenience during routine cleaning. You may also want advice on how to avoid messes, where to discard used soil, how to replace light tubes, etc. Discussing these issues ahead of time will help alleviate concerns the custodian may have about the safety or convenience of your new endeavor.

note: Appendix D describes how to build your own Grow Lab. It includes information on choosing fluorescent light fixtures. Prefabricated Grow Labs come with complete instructions for setting up the frame, the electrical components, and the covering. You can also purchase a Grow Lab supply kit that contains recommended seeds, containers, labels, growing mix, and fertilizer.

Finding the Right Location

If you have a tabletop GrowLab, or other light unit with a frame, place it on a sturdy table or counter at your students' eye level. The table should be strong enough to hold at least 100 pounds. Some teachers prefer to place the GrowLab in the center of the room where students can explore plants from all sides. Others place it against the wall where it takes up less space. The proximity of an electrical outlet is key. Don't place your garden too near a heat source, as this could dry out your crops.

You might think that placing your GrowLab near a window would offer needed supplementary sunlight, but a GrowLab's light system is specially designed to provide all the light plants normally need. Additional sunlight doesn't hurt, but if a window location also has hot and cold drafts, your plants will suffer.

If you have only one light fixture, supplementary window light can be beneficial. Suspend the lights from shelves, build a simple framework, or hang lights above a table or counter with chains attached to eyebolts in the ceiling. Again, avoid placing your garden too near a radiator or other heat source.

If you are gardening on the windowsill, see page 45 for information on window orientation and light availability.

Preparing the Base of Your Garden

We recommend that you use either moisture grids, perlite, or capillary matting in the base of an indoor garden.

The base material or tray acts as a reservoir to supply water and help maintain proper humidity for your plants. It also helps to keep soil moist on weekends and during vacations. (See page 47 for more on humidity and page 54 for more on vacation care.) Even windowsill plants benefit when you place them in trays with one of the base materials described below.

The prefabricated GrowLab units have trays with moisture grids. You can purchase these trays and moisture grids from the National Gardening Association to use in a homemade unit. The comparison that follows will help you decide which base material is best for you.

Comparing Indoor Garden Base Materials

Trays with Moisture Grids — Heavy-duty 22-by-11-by-2 ¾-inch Perma-Nest™ plastic trays with plastic insert grids are available from the National Gardening Association.

Advantages: They are easy to clean, long lasting, and hold enough water for at least a week. Plant roots can extend into the moisture grid without breaking when plants are removed. Fertilizer can also be dissolved in the water so plants can absorb nutrients through their roots.

When you pour perlite out, a cloud of dust which is irritating to respiratory passages will rise. Reduce this dust by pouring some water into the perlite first. Then pour the moistened perlite into the base. Cover your nose and mouth with a dust mask or cloth whenever you pour it.

Disadvantages: Plants can become saturated if too much water is added to the trays.

Perlite — Perlite is volcanic rock that has been expanded into a lightweight, white material by exposure to very high temperatures.

Advantages: It allows for good drainage if plants are over-watered. It is lightweight. Its color reflects light back onto plants. Plant roots can expand into the perlite and will lift without breaking when plants are removed. It's readily available in garden stores.

Disadvantages: Perlite dust, created when you pour perlite into the base of the garden, can irritate your lungs (wet it first or pour it into water to avoid this). It's hard to clean perlite when green algae or mold forms, so it is often replaced after one year.

Capillary Matting — This is a nonwoven fabric which, when placed under potted plants and dipped in a reservoir of water (e.g., plastic dishpan or pot) will wick water and provide a continuous supply of moisture for plants. Capillary matting is available from the National Gardening Association.

Advantages: It's easy to set up, relatively easy to clean, doesn't create a mess, can be reused, and is lightweight.

Disadvantages: Using capillary matting makes it somewhat more difficult to maintain adequate moisture during a long vacation. Plant roots sometimes grow into mats and break when removed (lift them every few days to avoid this). Some absorbency is lost each time the matting is washed.

Setting Up the Base

To hold whatever base material you choose, you'll need plastic trays that are at least 2 inches deep, or you'll need to line the base of your garden with 6-mil plastic. If you use plastic, make sure its edges extend at least 2 inches above where the bottom of the base meets the sides.

If you're using moisture grids with trays in the base of your garden, set the grids in the trays and fill the trays with water to the top of the grids. Plants grown in pots set on the grids will eventually stretch their roots into the water. You should have enough water to leave the plants for up to a week. Add more water to the trays when the soil in the pots begins to feel dry.

If you're using perlite in the base of your garden, pour 1 to 1½ inches (approximately 1 cubic foot) of moist perlite in the plastic-lined base or plastic tray. Add 2 to 3 gallons of water. This is about as moist as the material should be when you leave for the weekend or vacations.

If you have capillary matting, there are two ways to set it up:

> **If you have plastic growers' trays** or other 2- to 3-inch-deep trays as water reservoirs, lay a rigid piece of plastic, plexiglass, or foam over each tray, and cover it with capillary matting (see figure A). Allow the capillary matting to dip into the tray so several inches can be submerged in

water. Using this method, you should be able to maintain adequate water reserves for a week or so.

If you don't have plastic trays, lay the matting directly on the plastic in the base of your indoor garden and cut out a "wick" to draw water from a reservoir onto the mat (see figure B). The wick should be 4 inches wide and 10 inches long. Moisten the matting and the wick and place one end of the wick in the reservoir and one end under the matting. The wick must be firmly in contact with the matting. Although this system will work nicely for maintaining adequate water over long weekends, it's difficult to provide enough water in this way to last more than a week.

figure A

figure B

Choosing Fluorescent Tubes

We recommend using four to six fluorescent tubes in an 8-square-foot classroom indoor garden.

Owner-built GrowLabs are designed to accommodate six fluorescent tubes (two tubes in each of three fixtures) suspended over an 8-square-foot base. This setup provides adequate light for growing all classroom garden plants.

Cool white fluorescent tubes — the same as those used in most schools — will grow satisfactory plants indoors and are the least expensive tubes, although they should be replaced annually since their light intensity decreases with use. A mixture of cool white and warm white fluorescents provides a somewhat better quality of light for overall plant growth. (Warm refers to the light color, not temperature.) Wide-spectrum and full-spectrum light tubes provide light approximating sunlight, and they generally produce better growth, particularly as plants grow to maturity. These tubes are more expensive, but should provide a good light intensity for three years.

If you are gardening on a windowsill, or have only one fluorescent light fixture, you will not have the light intensity

note:

The special design of the light fixtures in prefabricated Grow Lab units allows for adequate light with only *four* fluorescent tubes.

Caution

Regardless of your base material and watering system, plants ideally should not be left unattended for more than a few days. During periods of active growth, plants use water rapidly and lights may need to be adjusted to prevent plants from growing into them.

required to bring some indoor crops to maturity, and all crops will take longer to grow. While single, two-tube fixtures are fine for raising many houseplants with low light needs, such as African violets or ferns, or for starting seedlings, most vegetable and flower crops need more light to mature. The Growers' Guide (Appendix A) indicates which crops are most appropriate for lower light levels.

Covering the Indoor Garden

Cover your GrowLab on the top and three sides with a polyethylene tent. You can create a tent from 4- or 6-mil clear polyethylene for a homemade unit. You'll need a piece of polyethylene for the front to cover the GrowLab during vacations. Prefabricated GrowLabs come with a climate control tent that is slit along the front edges.

First check with your custodian regarding local regulations, since some districts do not allow use of these materials in the classrooms. You can also use heavy-duty aluminum foil or Mylar, which will increase the amount of light available to your plants, but will limit viewing.

Although a covering is not absolutely necessary for growing plants, it will help maintain a comfortable humidity and adequate moisture (particularly during vacations) in your garden. Attach the covering to the edges of the frame, as illustrated below, with tacks, staples, or duct tape. Prefabricated tents slip easily over GrowLabs. You can remove the cover or just lift the front panel for better access and viewing, or to increase air circulation as needed. If your garden remains very wet or develops mold problems, you'll want to leave it uncovered or partially covered.

If you are gardening on the windowsill or using light fixtures without a frame, such a covering won't be feasible. You can, however, cover individual pots as described on page 54.

Caution

Be sure to attach the plastic inside the frame, on the side of the unit where electrical components are mounted. The electrical components should not be contained within the "tent," since the high humidity can cause the ground fault circuit interrupter to trip unnecessarily. Never lay a covering directly over light fixtures.

Cover front only during vacations

note:

The prefabricated GrowLab models include a clear, plastic climate control tent for covering the garden.

Choosing A Growing Medium

The growing medium in which you raise your plants is important. It provides a base to anchor the roots so the plants don't fall over. It also serves as a reservoir for water, air, and nutrients to be taken up through the roots.

We recommend using a commercial soilless potting mix, made from peat moss, vermiculite, and/or perlite, for a number of reasons:

It is light enough to allow for good water drainage, root aeration, and root movement, yet heavy and spongy enough to provide anchorage and to hold onto adequate water and nutrients.

It's easy to transport and readily available in most garden stores.

It's clean. It doesn't contain weed seeds, insects, or diseases that could flourish in the favorable conditions of an indoor garden.

It is a known quantity. While garden soil-based mixes may vary in pH and in nutrients, soilless mix contains few nutrients and has a good, stable pH. Through fertilizing, you can therefore control the nutrients that your plants receive.

It doesn't produce mud. If it gets on clothing, it brushes off easily.

It works. Thousands of schoolchildren, teachers, and commercial growers have achieved gardening success with this type of soilless mix.

Other Growing Mix Options

We suggest that beginning indoor gardeners start with a basic soilless mix. Once you have become confident of your indoor growing abilities, you can experiment with other types of mixes or additions to the basic mix.

Some people prefer to mix their own soilless or soil-based growing mix since it can be somewhat more economical. Some of the gardening references in Appendix E contain recipes for making these growing mixes. Below is a recipe for 8 gallons of a standard soilless growing mix.

Mix thoroughly:
4 gallons vermiculite
4 gallons sphagnum peat moss
4 tablespoons superphosphate (or 1 cup steamed bonemeal)
4 tablespoons dolomitic limestone

The following list outlines the benefits and drawbacks of adding garden soil, compost, or sand to your growing medium. When adding any of these materials, limit the quantity to one-third the volume of the mix.

Garden soil — Well-drained soil is the only type that should be added to a growing mix.

Advantages: Garden soil often has abundant nutrients, provides additional support, and holds water well.

Disadvantages: It has variable pH, may be too heavy, and can impede drainage. Because it is not sterile, it should ideally be pasteurized in a 180-degree oven for forty minutes. (This is a smelly process.)

Caution

Vermiculite, a common ingredient in potting mix, produces dust that can irritate respiratory passages. Wet your soilless mix before pouring to minimize dust, and pour carefully.

Compost—Sift compost through a screen before adding it to a growing mix.

Advantages: Compost has abundant nutrients, provides additional support, and holds water well.

Disadvantages: It has a variable pH and may not be sterile. If not properly composted, it should be pasteurized as described above.

Sand—Coarse builders' sand is best. Seashore sand may contain harmful salts.

Advantages: It provides additional support and improves drainage.

Disadvantages: Too much sand will cause a mix to dry out rapidly.

Selecting Containers

We recommend 6-inch-diameter plastic pots for use in classroom gardens for several reasons:

The pots are durable and can be washed and reused many times.

They do not dry out quickly like fiber or clay containers since they are not porous. This can be a particular benefit during school vacations. Plastic pots are also easy to clean and sterilize with a bleach solution.

They are relatively inexpensive and easily purchased in large quantities from garden stores and mail order suppliers.

They are large enough to accommodate the roots of most of the recommended indoor garden plants, particularly as the plants reach maturity.

Other Container Options

You need not feel limited to the type of container described above, since containers of other sizes or materials may be more accessible or appropriate. What follows is a comparison of various planting containers. Whichever you use, remember the following important points:

Most of the recommended indoor garden plants require at least a 6-inch soil depth to grow to maturity. (Check the Growers' Guide, Appendix A, for information on pot sizes for various crops.)

All containers must have drainage holes in the bottom to avoid waterlogging and killing plants. If necessary, punch drainage holes in the bottom of homemade containers before planting.

Market Packs—These are the standard plastic containers commonly used for seedlings in garden centers.

Advantages: They are readily available (you can easily find people who will donate them), easy to handle, and useful when growing seedlings for sale or to send home.

Disadvantages: They are too small to grow most plants to maturity.

DIGGING DEEPER What About pH?

The pH of the growing medium is an important consideration for growing plants. The pH reflects the acidity or alkalinity of a soil. The pH scale runs from 0 (acid) to 14 (alkaline), with 7.0 being a neutral pH.

The ideal range for growing most vegetable and annual flower plants is between 6.0 and 6.8. If the pH is not within a suitable range, plants cannot take up nutrients. In some cases, certain minerals increase to toxic levels in the soil if the pH is too low.

Commercial soilless mixes have a balanced pH in the appropriate range, so you won't have to be concerned with this when using them.

If you're using garden soil in your potting mix, measure the pH of your mix with a commercial test kit, available through sed companies and garden supply stores. (This is an excellent activity to do with students.) You can also use litmus paper to do a simple pH test. If the pH is too low (acid), raise it by adding 3 tablespoons of ground limestone for 8 gallons of potting mix. If it is too high, use a larger proportion of peat moss in your mix and test again.

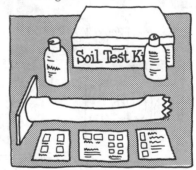

When cleaning pots or other garden equipment with bleach solution, take extra care, especially around children. Bleach is toxic and can burn skin and damage clothing.

School Milk Cartons – Be sure to make drainage holes.

Advantages: They are excellent for growing small plants for the children to take home and replant.

Disadvantages: They are too small for growing most plants to maturity.

Shallow Rectangular Growers' Flats – These may be wood or plastic.

Advantages: They are good for starting large quantities of closely spaced seeds for later transplanting; you can also use them as beds for growing crops like lettuce, or for starting houseplant cuttings.

Disadvantages: They are sometimes poorly drained.

Egg Cartons – Use the cardboard or plastic kind.

Advantages: These are fine for starting seedlings that will immediately be transplanted to larger containers.

Disadvantages: The cells are very small and dry out quickly.

Plastic Planting Bags – These are dark plastic bags filled with soil mix. The bags are perforated on top so that seeds can be sown or plants transplanted. They are available from many garden supply stores and catalogs.

Advantages: The plastic keeps the plant roots warm and moist, allowing good growth for heat-loving crops.

Disadvantages: They take up much space, are hard to reuse, and may not drain well.

Clay Pots – These come in many sizes.

Advantages: They allow very good air exchange, so there is less risk of mold problems. They are attractive. Their weight helps stabilize tall or bushy plants.

Disadvantages: They are fairly expensive and heavy, and are porous so they dry out very rapidly.

Fiber Pots – These come in a range of shapes and sizes.

Advantages: They are inexpensive and well aerated.

Disadvantages: They have a shorter life span than plastic or clay, and they dry out fairly rapidly.

Plastic Soda Bottle Bottoms – Many teachers have students bring in plastic 2-liter soda bottles. With the tops cut off, they become nice, deep, growing containers. Their most popular use is for small, individual terrariums (see page 71).

Advantages: They are readily available, free, and can provide good soil depth.

Disadvantages: They must be cut apart and are poorly drained. (Be sure to make holes.)

Chapter 3

Getting Started

Once your indoor garden is set up, you and your students will be eager to plant your crops. This chapter will help you plan your garden and prepare your planting equipment. Here you'll also find step-by-step sowing instructions and tips to help ensure germination.

DIGGING DEEPER | Curriculum Planning

What you decide to grow in your indoor garden will depend on your students' interests, your time and space limitations, and your curriculum goals. You might use the GrowLab as a context for plant growth experiments, for instance, or for thematic units on herbs, plant adaptations, rainforests, and so on. National Gardening Association's 307-page curriculum guide, *GrowLab: Activities for Growing Minds* will help you plan and facilitate age-appropriate GrowLab investigations that help students discover important life science concepts covering basic needs, reproduction, diversity, adaptations, and interdependence. See page 127 for information on this and other resources.

Planning

Many experienced gardeners have succumbed to the temptation of planting an entire package of radish seeds only to find, a month later, that they are the keepers of the largest radish plantations in town. Preliminary planning gives you control over your final harvest. The following are some important points to consider when planning your classroom garden.

What Can You Grow Indoors?

Included in the Growers' Guide (Appendix A) is a list of tried and true vegetables, flowers, and herbs that work well in the indoor garden. The crops recommended in the Growers' Guide generally do not take up much space. Most remain under 2 feet high. Most will produce abundantly when grown in 6-inch diameter pots.

You can also grow plants other than vegetables, herbs, and flowers indoors. An indoor garden is an excellent environment for starting all types of seedlings, cuttings, and bulbs. (See Chapter 6 for information on raising these.)

Remember, not all garden crops are good candidates for indoor growing. Corn, for instance, is too tall. Spinach is too sensitive to heat. Acorn squash takes up too much space.

What Do You Want To Grow?

This will depend on the role that you have chosen for your garden in the classroom. (Read Chapter 1, The Role of the Indoor Garden In Your Classroom, before planning your crops, since this may affect your choices.) We recommend that first-time indoor gardeners start small and try some relatively foolproof crops, such as radishes, lettuce, beans, marigolds, and dwarf tomatoes.

The planning stage of gardening offers an opportunity to involve the whole class in the decision-making process and to learn about the food likes and dislikes and ethnic backgrounds of the children. It makes sense to include some "sure-fire" crops and some of the class favorites. Some teachers include one or two experimental, unfamiliar items like peanuts or cotton for fun.

How Much and When Should You Plant?

Your Growers' Guide indicates the number of seeds of each recommended crop to plant in every pot, and the approximate number of weeks until maturity. Work backwards from your harvest plans and consider these questions:

How much of each crop will you need in the end? Consult the Growers' Guide (Appendix A) to determine the number of pots of each crop to plant. For instance, if you're planning a salad party for a class of thirty, assume that one small plant will feed each student. The Growers' Guide indicates that you can plant four lettuce plants per 6-inch pot, so you'll need to plant eight pots of lettuce. You can plan the same way for the rest of the salad vegetables.

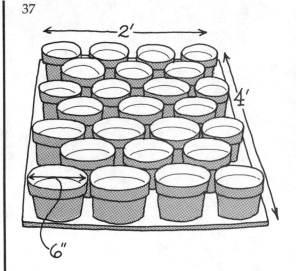

When do you want to have your harvest or finish your experiments? Once you've answered this question and used the Growers' Guide, you can determine when to plant each crop so it will be ready as needed. If you are planning for a coordinated harvest, remember that crops take different amounts of time to mature, so plan accordingly. (See Table 1 for a sample planning guide.)

Many teachers find it helpful to plan so that garden harvests and experiment conclusions occur just before a school vacation so they don't have to leave the classroom garden unattended.

How can you make best use of your growing space? Approximately twenty-five 6-inch pots can fit in a standard 2-by-4-foot Grow Lab at one time (although less may be desirable when the plants are large).

Think about planting dates and days to maturity to make maximum use of your space. Consider that with short-season crops, like radishes and lettuce, you'll be able to plant a second crop following in succession, or another short-season crop in the same pot, once the radishes are harvested.

Sample Planning Calendar

Some teachers find it helpful to draw up a full-year planning calendar for the indoor garden. A fourth-grade teacher drew up the following calendar to outline major garden activities and planting dates.

September — Assemble Grow Lab; write letters to seed companies; start houseplant cuttings for Thanksgiving gifts.

October — Conduct germination experiments; sow long-season crops (tomatoes, peppers, carrots) for Valentine's Day salad party; make sprouts for tasting; discuss World Food Day.

November — Start growth charts and records; begin fertilizer experiments; bring home houseplant gifts.

December — Sow more seeds for salad party (lettuce, cucumbers, beans); prepare garden for vacation; final reports on fertilizer experiments due.

January — Start marigold seeds for Mother's Day gifts; plant "mystery" seed; start nutrition unit; study pollination and hand pollinate cucumbers.

February — Design and produce menus for salad party; Valentine's Day harvest salad party.

March — Start seedlings for outdoor garden and spring plant sale; field trip to herb farm.

April — Transplant seedlings to larger containers; begin unit on water cycles.

May — Spring plant sale; bring home Mother's Day flowers; transplant seedlings outdoors.

June — Use proceeds from plant sale for field trip to botanical gardens. Clean and disassemble Grow Lab.

Planting

Once you've decided what to plant, how much of each crop to plant, and when to plant each one, you and the children will be ready to dive in. It's handy to set aside an area of the classroom for potting and planting, ideally close to a water source. In some classrooms, children cover their desks with newspaper or large plastic bags and prepare pots and plant seeds there.

When planting time comes, you'll either plant directly into permanent containers, or you'll plant thickly into containers from which you will transplant seedlings later.

Sowing Into Permanent Pots

You and your students will start some seeds in their permanent pots, either because they are crops that do not transplant well (see list below) or because you choose not to take the extra time to transplant with the class.

There are a number of plants whose tender root systems are shocked or damaged from transplanting. Although the classroom garden environment is more forgiving than the outdoors, and there is less chance of seedlings being set back by transplanting, the following crops should always be sown directly into their permanent containers:

beans   squash
peas   carrots
cucumbers   beets
melons   radishes

Sowing For Later Transplanting

You may want to sow seeds into temporary pots and transplant them later for a number of reasons:

Transplanting is an important and exciting gardening practice.

Tiny seeds are hard to handle and place where you want them. Scattering small seeds (like those of petunia and impatiens) and transplanting them later makes sense.

Transplanting can also be a space-saving activity. For instance, if your indoor garden is full and you want to start some seeds to take the place of maturing plants, sow them thickly in a shallow container and give them a head start. When you transplant them, you can choose only the healthiest ones so weaker plants won't take up space under the lights. If you want to start many cuttings and seeds for a plant sale or for children to take home, save space, and choose the nicest plants, by planting thickly and transplanting later.

Some plants actually benefit from transplanting. These include tomatoes, lettuce, peppers, and onions. Since a tomato plant develops small roots along its stem where the stem touches soil, transplanting it so its stem is deep in the soil increases root development. This, in turn, increases nutrient uptake and anchorage.

How to Plant Your Indoor Garden

1. **Gather your planting materials.**
   water source
   non-porous container (plastic bucket or plastic bag within a wastebasket for mixing the soilless mix)
   planting containers
   clean soilless or other potting mix*
   seed packets
   potting labels (either wooden popsicle sticks or plastic markers)
   waterproof marker or pencil
   watering bulb, watering can with sprinkling head, squeeze bottle, or plant mister

   *It's best not to reuse potting mix once you have already grown plants in it. In the warm, moist environment of the indoor garden, used potting mix may pass on disease or pest problems. You can reuse potting mix in compost piles or to repot house-plants or other well-established plants, which are less suscep-tible to pests and disease.

2. **Measure the amount of soilless mix that you'll need.** Use one of your 6-inch pots as a measure and put the mix into your mixing container. Throw in a little extra so you don't run short.

3. **Pour in about a third as much warm water as you have soil-less mix.** (The mixture is very absorbent and is much easier to work with when premoistened.) Continue adding water, mixing with your hands until the mixture is evenly moist throughout. Squeeze some in your hand. If water squeezes out, the mix is too wet. When properly moistened, the mix will form a ball in your hand and crumble when touched. If it's too wet, either add more mix, or leave the containers uncovered to let water evaporate.
   If you have the time, wet the mix and leave it overnight in a closed container to allow more complete absorption of water. If you can't use the moistened mix the next day, keep it covered so it doesn't dry. Don't use mix that has been moistened for more than a week, since it may begin to develop harmful fungus.

4. **If you are using pots that have very large drainage holes in the bottoms,** line just the bottom of each container with a single thickness of newspaper, newsprint, or paper towel. This will prevent the potting mix from falling out through the drainage holes. Don't use shiny newspaper or maga-zines, as some of the coatings used on these are toxic. Don't leave the paper sticking up above the soil in the pot, as this "wicks" moisture away from the soil and plants.

5. **Fill the container with moistened mix.** Press the mix down lightly with your hand or another container and leave at least 1 inch of headroom at the top. This space will make watering easier later on, and will allow you to add mix later, to help bury root crops and stabilize stems.

6. **Sow the seeds.**
   If seeds are extremely fine, sprinkle them on the soil surface

note:

If you're using slow-release fertilizer (see page 49), the best time to add it is when you are mixing the water and potting mix. This will distribute the fertilizer evenly.

figure A

figure B

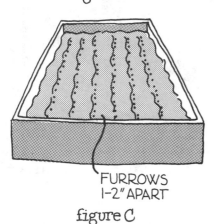

FURROWS
1-2" APART

figure C

figure D

and pat them into the soil (see figure A). To ensure a better distribution, mix them first with sand or a little potting mix. **If they are larger,** sow them in shallow furrows or individual small holes. The general rule is to plant seeds at a depth of three times the diameter of the seed.

If you are sowing seeds directly into their permanent containers, refer to the Growers' Guide and space the correct number of seeds evenly around the pot (see figure B). Because it is unreasonable to expect 100 percent germination from a batch of seed, put two seeds in each planting hole.

If you are planting closely for later transplanting, space the seeds ¼ inch apart in rows 1 to 2 inches apart (see figure C). You will be transplanting the seedlings while they're still small, before the roots get too large to intertwine. (See page 51 for more on transplanting.)

7. **Cover the seeds with soil unless they are fine.** Pat them down to ensure maximum contact, and thus maximum conduction of water, between soil and seed.

8. **Moisten the soil again carefully with a plant mister, squeeze bottle, or gentle sprinkling head** (to avoid washing the seeds away).

9. **Make a wooden, plastic, or masking tape label.** Using a waterproof marker or pencil, list the date, the variety planted, and, if appropriate, the name or initials of the student doing the planting.

10. **Cover the container with clear plastic or wax paper** (see figure D). This will create a greenhouse effect and maintain moist conditions during germination. Do not let the covering rest on the soil, or the tender seedlings will be pulled out when it's removed. To avoid this, prop up the covering with pot labels or toothpicks.

11. **Place the containers in the indoor garden or another warm spot in the room.** If your room is very cold, or your planting area is near cold windows, you can put the containers near, but never on, a heat source (radiator, ducts) provided they don't get too hot and dry. Containers do not have to be under lights at this point, but you will need to place them under lights or by a sunny window as soon as the seeds germinate.

12. **Store leftover seeds in a sealed container** (film canister, glass jar, envelope) and keep them in a cool, dry place until you need them. You can place seed envelopes in a glass jar in the refrigerator with corn meal or rice to absorb moisture. If stored properly, most seeds will keep for several years. Your class can perform germination tests to check the viability of seeds before planting.

Germination Secrets

Seeds have particular requirements that must be met if they are to successfully germinate (sprout). The two that will most concern you are warmth and moisture.

Moisture

Keep seeds in your indoor garden constantly moist until they germinate. Cover the container with clear plastic or wax paper while the seeds are germinating. This will maintain warmth and moisture, and will allow the children to watch what is happening. Again, don't let the covering touch the soil. If the soil mix seems to be drying out, water with a plant mister or very gentle watering head to avoid washing seeds away.

Check containers daily. Remove the covering as soon as seedlings sprout and set the containers under lights. Begin to water seedlings as described on page 47.

Warmth

A Grow Lab, warm windowsill, or spot near a heating source will provide adequate warmth for the germination of most indoor garden plants. You won't need to carefully monitor germination temperatures for different plants although seeds do germinate at different minimum, optimum, and maximum temperatures.

If you have a classroom where temperatures fall below 50 degrees for extended periods of time over weekends or vacations, consider using a heating cable (see Appendix D) or a propagating mat (available at many garden centers or through supply catalogs) in the base of your garden. These will provide adequate temperatures for germination.

Table 5 lists the range of germination temperatures for a selection of common indoor garden vegetables. This table will help your students predict when their seeds will germinate. You can use this information to have students place "bets" and turn their predictions into a game.

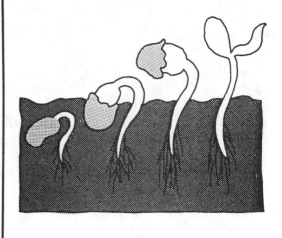

Caution

Never place containers directly on top of fluorescent lights, radiators, or other heating or electrical devices.

Germination Temperatures for Selected Vegetables			Table 5
	Minimum	Ideal Range	Maximum
Beans	60 degrees	70-85 degrees	95 degrees
Beets	40	65-75	95
Carrots	40	60-70	95
Cucumbers	60	70-80	105
Lettuce	35	45-65	85
Peppers	60	70-75	95
Tomatoes	50	70-75	95

42

Table 6 illustrates the effect of soil temperature on the rate of seed germination, using carrots as an example. With a soil thermometer purchased at a garden supply store, or through one of the suppliers listed in Appendix E, the class can conduct experiments to test the effect of temperature on the germination of other crops, too.

Effect of Soil Temperature on Rate of Germination (Carrots)	Table 6
Temperature - Degrees Fahrenheit	Days to Germination
95	8.6
77	6.2
68	6.9
50	17.3
41	50.6

Germination Tests

To see if old seeds are worth replanting, conduct germination tests with your class. For each type of seed being tested, lay out ten seeds on a moist paper towel. Fold up the moist towel like an accordion, moisten again, and place it in a plastic bag.

After a week or ten days, unroll each towel and have children count the number of seeds, out of ten, that have germinated. Then calculate a percentage of germination. If less than 50 percent have germinated, use fresh seed or sow seed more heavily, to compensate for the low germination rate.

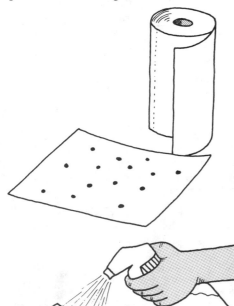

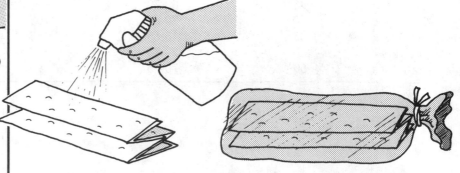

Light

Most of your seeds will sprout with or without light. Children should carefully observe containers, however, since they'll need to place the seedlings under lights as soon as they emerge from the soil.

Germination Failure

There are a number of reasons why seeds may fail to germinate. If you have a problem with germination, refer to this list:

Soil temperature too low or too high
Soil dried out
Seeds planted too deeply
Seeds washed away during watering
Seeds too old and/or improperly stored
Poor soil-to-seed contact
Damping off disease

Don't become discouraged if you have poor germination. Start with clean containers and fresh mix and plant again. Don't delay. You will probably be successful on your second try. Remember also that some seeds germinate very quickly and others take longer, so check the Growers' Guide for approximate germination times.

Chapter 4

Maintaining a
Healthy Environment

Whether you're gardening on a windowsill, under a two-tube fluorescent light fixture, or in a Grow Lab garden laboratory, the environment must meet specific plant needs if your plants are to thrive. This chapter describes those basic needs and explains how to meet them in your indoor garden.

Although different plants have specific needs for ideal growth, you will maintain conditions that may be a compromise, offering an average of what most plants will need for reasonable growth, within your setting. (Consult your Growers' Guide, Appendix A, for information on expected yields in an indoor garden.)

Remember, there are a number of lessons to be learned from failures as well as successes in the garden. Even with the most careful garden management, plants sometimes fail to thrive. Accidents happen. Pests or diseases cause crop failure. Seeds may fail to germinate. But a failure of one sort or another can become the focus for a new lesson or experiment. For example, if your beans develop a mold and the plants die, seize the opportunity to investigate the life of molds. Use magnifying glasses and microscopes to examine them. Find out what conditions they need to thrive. Try growing molds on different substances. Learn about helpful molds.

Do not angle the lights so that one end is higher than the other. This is unsafe since water could condense and run down to the light terminal, creating the danger of electric shock.

Light Intensity

Intensity is an important aspect of light affecting plant growth and development. The other important factors are color (spectrum) and duration. See pages 90 through 92 in the curriculum guide, GrowLab: Activities for Growing Minds for a thorough explanation of these key factors.

Most of the flowers, vegetables, and herbs that you'll grow indoors do quite well with the 1,000 to 1,500 footcandles of light provided by six fluorescent tubes, and some will do well with quite a bit less. (A footcandle is the amount of light produced in a totally dark space by one candle shining on a white surface that is 1 square foot in size, 1 foot from the candle.) By contrast, 500 footcandles is average office light, and the light at noon on a sunny day might be as bright as 10,000 foodcandles.

The amount of light that your indoor garden receives will depend on many factors, including the time of year, orientation of the window, and proximity of lights to a reflective surface. Placing your light garden near a white wall or backing it with aluminum foil increases, through reflection, the amount of light available to your plants. You and the children can investigate various ways to increase the light available to your plants. Use a light meter to check your efforts (see Digging Deeper, page 46).

Light

One of the most critical factors for your indoor plants is light. Using the right type and number of tubes, as described on page 30, will not, by itself, ensure success. It's important that you follow the height and duration recommendations in this section to provide adequate light for a thriving garden.

Adjusting Light Height

Always keep the lights 3 to 6 inches from the tops of the plants to foster good plant growth. The amount of light reaching your plants drops drastically as you raise the lights, so resist the temptation to keep lights high for good viewing. If your lights are on adjustable chains, you can raise them easily while children are watering, inspecting plants, or conducting investigations. If your plants are very tall and spindly looking, your lights are probably too high.

Since you will have plants of varying heights but will still want to maintain light at the proper distance, you should arrange plants according to height with some lights higher than others. Another way to adjust height is to place shorter plants on top of upturned pots.

Light intensity is much greater at the center of your tubes than at the several inches on either end and greater in the middle of the Grow Lab than near the edges. Rotate your plants every couple of weeks to ensure that all plants have a chance to receive adequate lighting.

Controlling Light Duration

Plug your lights into a timer so you can control them automatically, and leave them on for fourteen to sixteen hours per day. Leaving the lights on continually will not cause plants to produce more abundantly. Plants actually require a period of darkness each day in order for respiration to occur. Respiration, which takes place primarily at night, is the process whereby plants convert the products of photosynthesis into usable energy.

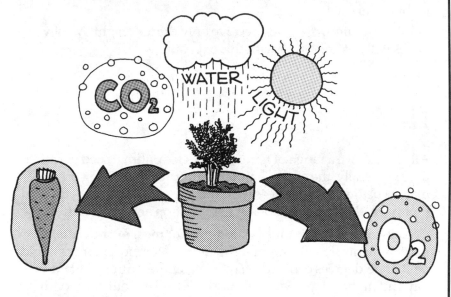

Windowsill Light

The amount of light that your plants receive on a windowsill depends on the direction the window faces, whether the sun is blocked by trees or a building, the number of cloudy days, and how much overhang your roof has. Another consideration with windowsill plants is the duration of light. During most of the school year, even the best south-facing window will receive fewer than the fourteen to sixteen hours we recommend.

Given the light limitations of most windowsill gardens, it's best to stick with leaf and root vegetables here. Since we don't eat the fruits of these vegetables, it's not necessary to have the high level or longer duration of light required to induce flowering in many plants. Crops recommended for windowsill gardens include:

beets	radishes
carrots	tomatoes
garlic	herbs
lettuce	flowering bulbs
mustard	houseplants
onion tops	fruit seeds

On a sill, light comes from only one direction, so you'll need to rotate your plants every couple of days as they begin to lean toward the light. Your class can investigate this movement toward light, called "phototropism." Set up experiments indoors and identify the process outdoors in the environment.

Although many factors determine the amount of light available to windowsill plants, the following describes the lighting conditions of different windowsill orientations.

DIGGING DEEPER — Understanding Photosynthesis

Life on earth is completely dependent on the food and oxygen produced by plants and a few other organisms during the process of photosynthesis.

Photosynthesis is the process by which plants containing green chlorophyll employ the energy of light to combine carbon dioxide (CO_2) from the air with hydrogen (H) from water (H_2O) to produce sugars.

The relatively simple sugars, produced through photosynthesis, are later built into more complex plant foods such as starches, fats, and proteins.

Some of the food produced by a plant during photosynthesis is temporarily stored in the leaves. The remainder is transported through the stem to other parts of the plant where it is stored until needed. This food energy might be stored in a number of forms —as a starch (in potatoes) or as a fat (in peanuts), for example.

The plant eventually uses the stored food to produce more foliage, roots, stems, flowers, and ultimately, to produce offspring, thus beginning the cycle again.

Many of your teaching materials have further explanations of photosynthesis and respiration. Use those references to make these concepts part of your Grow Lab lessons.

How Plants Can Live in an Enclosed System

CLASSROOM PROFILE After helping to build a class terrarium, one thoughtful fifth-grade student asked, "If we need oxygen (which plants give off) and plants need carbon dioxide (which we give off), how can plants survive in an enclosed terrarium?" If you study the cycles described above, you'll notice that plants both photosynthesize *and* respire. During respiration they produce the carbon dioxide that they need for photosynthesis. (The decay of plant matter also produces carbon dioxide.) Thus, technically, we cannot live without them, but they can live perfectly well without us!

Measuring Light Intensity

CLASSROOM PROFILE

One class of eighth-grade students used the light meter in a camera to measure the intensity (footcandles) of light available to plants in various parts of the room and at various distances from the tubes. This is the procedure they used:

Set the film speed at ASA 200 and the shutter speed at 1/125 second. Aim the camera at a white sheet of paper where your plants will be located. Get close enough so the meter records only light reflected from the paper. Be careful not to create shadows.

Focus on the paper and adjust the f-stop until a correct exposure shows in the light meter of the camera. F-stops will equal approximate footcandles as follows:

F-stop	Footcandles
2.8	32
4.0	64
5.6	125
8.0	250
11.0	500
16.0	1,000
22.0	2,000

Good!

DIGGING DEEPER

Cool and Warm Weather Crops

In outdoor gardens, we distinguish between cool and warm weather crops. As the terms indicate, cool season crops are those which produce best growth, or will mature only during cool temperatures (40 to 65 degrees). Warm season crops require warmer temperatures (above 65) for best growth. Since classroom temperatures tend to be warm, there are certain cool weather crops, like spinach and peas, that can be quite difficult to grow indoors. Others, like lettuce, will grow nicely indoors but may become bitter with temperatures that are too warm. *Continued next page*

Eastern windows – These receive two to four hours of morning sun. Reserve these locations for growing radishes, lettuce and other leafy vegetables, root vegetables, and houseplants that require minimal light.

Southern windows – These receive full sun during most of the day and are a good choice for growing all of the windowsill crops. Plants can, however, get too hot, dry out quickly, and scorch on an unshaded southern windowsill.

Western windows – These generally receive good light for about eight hours a day.

Northern windows – These receive only diffused light. Most vegetables will not grow well with this exposure.

Heat

All plants have a range of temperatures for optimal seed germination. Generally, the optimal air temperature for growing the mature plants is slightly less than that for germinating seeds. (See page 41 for information on germination and temperature.)

The 60- to 80-degree range is adequate for most of your indoor garden plants. Ideally, night temperatures for most plants should be 10 to 15 degrees cooler than the day temperatures. Both of these day and night ranges will typically be found in your classroom climate. The plastic or foil covering that you use to maintain humidity in your indoor garden (see page 31) will also help to maintain somewhat higher than room temperatures.

In extremely cold situations, such as over a vacation when the heat is off, you can use a heating cable to maintain heat in your classroom garden. If using a heating cable, do so only for germination or to maintain a reasonable temperature in the garden. Too much heat can cause plants to dry quickly. Remember, when using a heating cable, always keep the base material moist. (See Appendix D for information on how to set up a heating cable.)

Water

Plants need water because it carries nutrients through the soil, into the roots, and up through the plant to places where the nutrients can be used. Plants use water as a raw material in photosynthesis. Water also helps to keep the plants erect, enabling them to take full advantage of light for photosynthesis.

Too little water will cause wilting, decrease nutrient transport and photosynthesis, and will lead to death of the plant.

Too much water will prevent air exchange around the roots, which essentially suffocates them and leads to rotting of the roots. (Roots that have to search a little for water will become stronger than those that are overwatered.)

Overwatering can cause at least as many problems with your plants as underwatering.

Watering Your Garden

It's best to water only when the plants need it rather than on a set schedule. Large plants with lots of leaves use water faster than small plants. Porous planting containers, like clay pots, will lose water much more quickly than solid (plastic) containers. The soil will dry out more quickly when classroom temperatures are high. If you use a heating cable (see Appendix D), pay particular attention when it is on.

To tell when your plants need water, stick your finger about an inch into the soil in a pot. If soil adheres to it and/or feels moist, you do not need to water yet. Be sure to check a number of pots. Some classes purchase water meters at garden stores and compare the instrument readings with the students' own subjective readings.

When you water, give each plant enough to wet the soil thoroughly. Add water until it comes out from the bottom of the pot.

When watering young seedlings, use only a gentle sprinkling head or a squeeze bottle to avoid washing them away.

(See page 54 for information on providing water during vacations.)

Controlling Your Garden's Humidity

The humidity in your classroom will fluctuate a great deal. Winter conditions indoors tend to be dry. The ideal humidity for the plants in your indoor garden is between 50 and 70 percent. You will not have to keep a careful eye on the specific humidity, but rather, notice and respond to the signs of extremes in humidity. You can purchase a humidity gauge from a hardware store to measure and experiment with humidity's effect on plant growth.

Regularly moisten the base material in your gardening unit to maintain proper humidity.

Moisten it during the week when watering, and let it dry out somewhat between waterings. Constant moisture could create disease problems. Before a weekend or vacation, provide a reservoir of water as described on page 54.

If you have a windowsill garden, keep a tray with a moistened base material (sand, perlite, gravel, capillary matting) under your plants. If the air is very dry, keep plants close together as they help provide humidity for each other. Enclose windowsill plants in large plastic bags if you plan to be away for an extended period of time.

Keep the covering on the top and three sides of your Grow Lab. If your Grow Lab shows signs of excessive humidity, lift all or part of the covering to provide better air circulation.

Table 7 lists symptoms of an excess or deficiency of humidity and offers suggestions for addressing these problems.

Continued . . .

All of the crops listed in the Growers' Guide have been successfully grown in an indoor environment. If you have very extreme temperature conditions in your classroom, choose crops accordingly. Below is a list of some common cool and warm weather crops that you can grow:

Cool	Warm	
peas	tomatoes	cucumber
radishes	peppers	marigolds
lettuce	eggplant	basil
carrots	beans	zinnias
snapdragons	peanuts	

Water and electricity don't mix. Raise lights when watering so that watering is done beneath, not above, light fixtures. Some teachers prefer to remove pots from the garden during watering. If fixtures do get wet, unplug or turn off the lights immediately. Dry lights thoroughly before you turn them on again.

If you're using a heating cable, as described in Appendix D you should keep the base material constantly moist, since this will help conduct the heat to the root zone of the plants.

Regulating Humidity	Table 7
Humidity Too High	Humidity Too Low

Symptoms:
White fungus or green algae growth on soil or base material

How to lower humidity:
Partially remove covering (plastic or foil) from your garden to increase air circulation.

Let the base material in the garden dry out.

Cut back on your frequency of watering.

Thin plants (don't crowd them).

Create breezes (open window, run fan, etc.).

Symptoms:
Leaves curling downward, tips brown

How to raise humidity:
Keep the garden covered with plastic or foil.

Keep the base material constantly moist (not soaked).

Keep a number of pots clustered together.

If you do not have a Grow Lab, set your pots of plants in a container filled with 1 inch of pebbles, perlite, or sand and keep them moist.

Mist plants every few days.

note:

Some people prefer misting to other methods of raising humidity. Its effect on raising humidity, however, is only temporary. Misting does help clean dust from plant pores. If you mist, do so lightly and early in the day. (Wet foliage at night can create pest and disease problems.) Do not mist plants that have hairy leaves and stems, such as tomatoes and African violets.

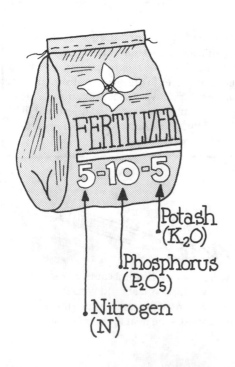

Potash (K$_2$O)

Phosphorus (P$_2$O$_5$)

Nitrogen (N)

Nutrients

For healthy growth, all plants require certain nutrients that normally come from the soil. The three primary nutrients are nitrogen (N), phosphorus (P), and potassium (K). There are other essential nutrients that are equally important but plants require them in much smaller amounts. (See Table 8 for information on nutrient functions.) Although soilless mixes generally contain some nutrients to get plants off to a good start, you and your students will have to provide additional fertilizer to your plants on a regular basis.

We recommend a complete water-soluble liquid fertilizer for use with indoor gardens for several reasons:

It is widely available in garden stores and catalogs.

It is relatively inexpensive.

It is rapidly available to plants and the concentration can be easily controlled.

The three numbers on a fertilizer container (5-10-5, for example), represent the percentages of nitrogen (5 percent), phosphorus (10 percent), and potassium (5 percent) in an available form in that particular fertilizer. A complete fertilizer is one that contains all of these three primary plant nutrients. Use a fertilizer with equal amounts of nitrogen, phosphorus, and potassium, such as 10-10-10, or with a higher percentage of phosphorus, such as 15-30-15.

Fertilizing Your Garden

Follow the directions on the fertilizer container to determine proper dilution and frequency of fertilizing. Overfertilizing can be as harmful as underfertilizing.

The dilution rate will vary greatly with the type of fertilizer. Manufacturers of most liquid and water-soluble fertilizers recommend that you fertilize every two weeks with a full strength dose. Some teachers prefer fertilizing with one-fourth the suggested strength every time they water. This requires less attention than remembering when to fertilize. It's often convenient to mix up a large batch of fertilizer in plastic gallon milk jugs and pour that into the watering can as needed.

Start fertilizing plants only after the third leaf appears on the plant. The first two "leaves" or cotyledons are actually a part of the seed and contain nutrients to support early development of the plant.

Other Fertilizer Options

There are other types of fertilizers that you can use in an indoor garden. Below is a description and comparison of fertilizer alternatives.

Organic Liquid Fertilizers—Fish emulsion, seaweed, and combinations of these are commonly used fertilizers. The proportions of nutrients are lower than in synthetic fertilizers, but the instructions for application will compensate for that.

Advantages: They are rapidly available to plants but less concentrated so there is less chance of overfertilizing.

Disadvantages: Most of these have a disagreeable smell. They will be more expensive in the long run than other water soluble liquids.

Slow-Release Fertilizers—These are generally beads of fertilizer that are initially mixed in with soil as it is moistened, or applied on the surface after planting. Most brands continue to release nutrients for three to four months or more, depending on heat and moisture. The more often you water the plants, the more quickly fertilizer is released. Warm water also hastens fertilizer release.

Advantages: They require no attention or additional fertilizing for three or four months after the initial mixing.

Disadvantages: Young children may be tempted to put beads into their mouths. (The beads are toxic.) The availability of nutrients is less controlled and they will run out with very long-term crops. (You can then add additional fertilizer beads, or water with a liquid fertilizer.) There is a danger of overfertilizing plants and causing a buildup of harmful fertilizer salts if you use too much water, or water that's too warm.

Compost or Soil in Potting Mix—While soilless mixes have many advantages, potting mixes that also contain some compost or soil are commonly used.

Advantages: Compost and soil contain many trace elements and beneficial organisms, are less expensive than commercial ferti-

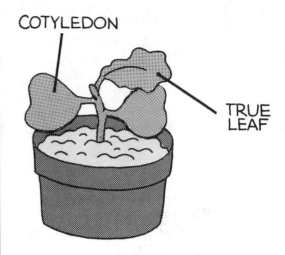

COTYLEDON

TRUE LEAF

Caution

Fertilizer is made of concentrated chemicals that can be dangerous if taken internally. Blue, water-soluble fertilizer might be a particular temptation to young gardeners. Slow-release fertilizers are easily ingestible beads and could also be a hazard. Store these supplies out of the reach of children, and discuss these safety issues early on with the class. If fertilizer is ingested, do not induce vomiting unless advised to do so by a doctor or poison center. Rinse the child's mouth thoroughly with water and call a poison center immediately.

50

lizers, and more closely approximate outside soil conditions.

Disadvantages: They increase the possibility of pest and disease problems and can make the mix too heavy. You will have less precise control over nutrient amounts. You'll need to pasteurize compost and soil by heating small batches in an oven at 180 degrees for thirty to forty minutes. (This decreases nutrient availability and smells bad.)

Nutrient Troubleshooting

Table 8 outlines the functions and symptoms of deficiencies and excesses of the three major plant nutrients. The table simplifies what are actually very complex nutrient functions.

If you are using a complete fertilizer and are using too little or too much, the problem will be most apparent as a deficiency or excess of nitrogen.

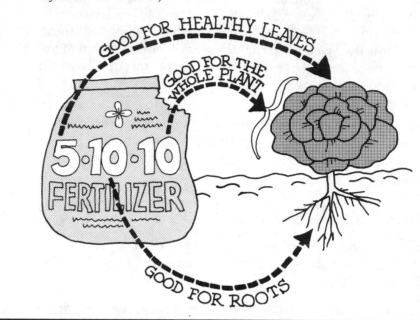

Nutrient Functions and Deficiency and Excess Symptoms — Table 8

Nutrient	Function	Deficiency Symptoms	Excess Symptoms
Nitrogen (N)	necessary for foliage, growth	yellowing of leaves, beginning with the youngest	long, weak stems and lush, thin foliage, failure to flower
Phosphorus (P)	necessary for root growth, flowering, and fruiting	development of deep green or purplish hue on lower leaves	(not apparent)
Potassium (K)	contributes to overall vigor and resistance	slow growth, stunting, and browning of leaves	(not apparent)

Transplanting

Transplanting is the process of removing young plants from containers in which you first planted them and transferring them into new, generally larger containers. Remember, some crops should never be transplanted. (See page 24 for information on which crops withstand transplanting.) Carefully transplanting plants into new, more comfortable homes can be a thrilling experience for youngsters. Make sure that you read through the following steps to increase transplanting success.

How To Do It

1. **Don't transplant until the seedlings show their first true leaves** after the first two seed leaves (cotyledons) have appeared. The cotyledons provide food to the plant until the true leaves are available to make food through photosynthesis. A week or so after the cotyledons have appeared, you'll see a true leaf that is more characteristic of the plant. Once these true leaves appear, it's time to transplant. You can wait a couple of weeks, but don't wait much longer because roots will develop and intertwine, making it difficult to lift out seedlings without some damage to the roots.

2. **Prepare the containers into which you will transplant seedlings.** Clean previously used containers with a bleach solution of ½ cup bleach to 1 gallon of water and rinse them with clear water to remove any bleach residue. Fill containers with pre-moistened soilless mix, leaving an inch of head room.

3. **Use your finger or a pencil to make planting holes in the soil.** Holes should be deep enough to accommodate the fully extended roots of the seedlings, and wide enough to allow you to lower these seedlings into the holes.

4. **Grasp a seedling by one of the seed leaves.** (If a seed leaf is torn off, the plant won't be harmed.) Pulling on the leaf gently, coax the seedling out of the soil with a pencil, potting label, toothpick, or similar tool. Don't grasp the seedling by the stem. The stem may seem stronger than the seed leaf, but it is much more important to the plant. If the stem is damaged, circulation to the upper part of the plant is shut off and the plant dies.

5. **Lower the seedling into a planting hole.** Use the pencil or potting label to tease the roots down into the hole. Help the roots to spread out as much as possible.

6. **Press the potting mix around and into the hole with your fingers or potting tool.**

7. **Water the pot thoroughly once it is completely planted.** This gives the plant plenty of water to start with and also helps pack the potting mix around the roots.

8. **Put a label in the pot to identify variety and dates of planting and transplanting.**

A Creative Lesson on Thinning

One second-grade teacher used role playing to teach children about the difficult task of thinning. She had a group of eight children stand very close together in front of the room and asked them to imagine that they were lettuce plants growing very tightly in a pot. She asked some on the outside to bend and cast a shadow over the others and told the eight "plants" that they would have one glass of water and one sandwich to share among themselves.

The "lettuce plants" were then asked how it felt to be so tightly packed; to share that small amount of food and water. How long did they think they could survive like that? The children then began to relate this to the discussion of plants. One of the other students then selected five of the "plants" to thin out and transplant to other pots. Then all the "plants" stretched out and described what it felt like to have room to grow!

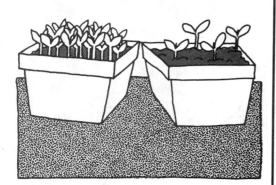

Thinning

Thinning involves removing some plants from groups that are growing close together to allow the remaining plants more room and better conditions for growth. Thinning, both in outdoor and indoor gardens, is an often overlooked and disliked task. After all, how can we bear to pull out any of our precious, carefully tended seedlings?

Failure to thin plants is a common reason for poor plant growth in both indoor and outdoor gardens. Plants growing too closely together will compete with one another for water and nutrients. They'll all suffer and you will not have healthy plants or a harvest if you don't thin them. Crowded plants also suffer from decreased air circulation and increased risk of disease and pest problems.

The sooner you thin, the better. The longer you wait, the more time the plants will have had to compete, the harder it will be to avoid disturbing the other plants, and the more attached you and the children will have gotten to the plants.

How To Do It

1. **Look for the healthiest looking plants and thin out the rest.** Do this as soon as it's obvious that you have too many plants crowded together (once the first true leaves have formed). Check your Growers' Guide (Appendix A) to see how many plants should remain in each container, and thin to that number. Teachers should carefully oversee the thinning process, since it's easy to become overzealous or careless when thinning.

2. **The most benign way to thin crops that can be transplanted is to transplant them into other containers.** If you don't have room in the class to keep them, you can give them as gifts to other classrooms or send them home with the children.

   Another method of thinning is to cut off the unwanted plants with your fingernail just above the soil line. The bottom of the plant will eventually die. This is preferable to pulling out plants to be thinned, since the pulling may disturb the roots of other plants.

3. **Add additional soilless mix to the pot if you have thinned root crops like radishes, turnips, or carrots.** Add enough to cover the roots (they tend to heave up out of the soil in this light mix). This will improve the root quality at harvest. Exposed roots become dry and scaly.

4. **Water again.** You may have disturbed plant roots during thinning.

5. **Your class can enjoy eating the resulting thinnings** if the plants, like lettuce, mustard, beets, parsley, onions, or herbs, have edible leaves. No sense in letting the products of your labors go to waste!

Pollination

Pollination is the process by which pollen from the tip of the stamen (called the anther) of a male flower is transferred to the tip of the pistil (called the stigma) of a female flower so that fertilization, and then fruit and seed production, can occur, thus completing the full cycle in the life of a plant. (See Flower Power in Appendix B.)

In a garden, pollination is only necessary for those crops that produce edible fruit or seeds. If we eat the root or leaves of a plant (as with carrots and lettuce) there is no need for pollination in order to achieve a harvest. Crops like cucumbers and tomatoes, that produce edible fruit or seeds, must somehow be pollinated in order to produce a harvest. In nature, pollination is most often aided by the action of wind and insects.

Most flowers are bisexual, that is, they have stamens and pistils in the same blossom. (These are called "perfect" flowers.) Pollination occurs easily in perfect flowers since their parts are arranged to enable pollen to transfer easily. The slightest touch or air movement around most perfect flowers will lead to pollination. Indoor garden crops that have perfect flowers and require only slight movement to pollinate themselves include tomatoes, peppers, eggplant, peas, and beans.

Some species, such as cucumbers and squash, have separate male and female blossoms, called "imperfect" flowers. You can recognize the female blossoms by the miniature fruit (ovary) that develops behind them, even before pollination occurs.

In your indoor garden, cucumbers are the only crop that you should pollinate by hand to simulate the role of bees.

Pollinating Cucumbers Indoors

Since there are (hopefully!) no bees in your classroom to carry the pollen from the male to the female flowers of your cucumbers, you and the children must fill that role. To do this, you'll need to distinguish the male flower from the female flower. As the plants flower, you will notice that some of the blossoms have a miniature fruit (ovary) at the base. These are the female flowers.

Although this miniature fruit looks like the beginning of a cucumber, it won't continue to develop unless it's pollinated. Male flowers are generally the first to appear and they do so in greater numbers than the female flowers. Male flowers don't have a miniature fruit at the base of the blossom. Once you have some female flowers, you can try your hand at pollination.

Using a small paintbrush, carefully collect the yellow pollen grains from the tip of the stamen (the anther) on the male flower, and gently touch the brush to the tip of the pistil (the stigma) of the female flower. As long as some of the yellow pollen is transferred to the female, you're likely to achieve pollination. Female flowers that have not been pollinated will die.

Pollination Adaptations

An exciting concept for children is that the primary "purpose" in the life of a flower is to become pollinated. Flowers all have adaptations such as color, size, shape, fragrance, etc., to attract bees and other pollinators (or assure pollination by wind or other means). The pollinator uses the sweet nectar and pollen to make food for itself and its young. While collecting pollen, the bee or other pollinator inadvertently transfers pollen from one flower to another.

Many flowers (such as grasses) are small and inconspicuous, while others (cucumbers, roses, etc.) are showy, bright, and fragrant. Flowers that are wind-pollinated need to be light and airy while flowers that need to attract insects must be bright, fragrant, and flamboyant!

Have your students study flowers from outdoors, from home, and from the classroom garden. Use magnifying glasses to examine them and try to identify some of the flower parts. (Not all flowers will have all of the parts shown in the diagram in Appendix B.) Feel some stigmas to see if they are sticky and have children guess why this might be. Ask students to describe the characteristics of flowers that assist in pollination.

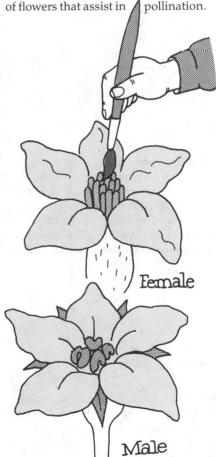

Female

Male

Preparing for a Vacation

After carefully tending your indoor school garden for weeks or months, you may find yourself worrying about having to leave it for a week or more because of a school vacation. Some teachers avoid this problem altogether by planning the calendar so that garden projects end just before a vacation and new ones begin afterward. Others choose to carry plants through a vacation.

Certainly, the more attention plants get during a vacation, the more likely they'll survive and thrive. Consider enlisting a custodian or teacher to check the water and light heights a couple of times during a vacation. In any case, there are some simple steps you can take to increase the chances of your plants surviving for a week or more with little or no care. The most important step you can take is to make sure that the soil around them remains moist. During a vacation, the most serious problem you must guard against is drought. Here is what you can do to prevent it:

1. **If you have perlite in the base of your garden, fill it with water that nearly touches your pots.** (Two to three gallons should be plenty.) This water will evaporate during the vacation, keeping the humidity in your garden high. High humidity reduces water loss from your plants.

    If you are using capillary matting on top of trays as illustrated on page 30, fill the tray with water, moisten the matting, and dip the ends of the matting in the water to act as a wick. Water will be drawn up continually, providing humidity for the plants.

    If you are using matting directly on the plastic liner, fill a large container with water and wet your capillary matting wick and fabric. Place one end of the wick in the reservoir and the other end under the matting, ensuring good contact with the mat. If you have room, your best bet is to leave the reservoir inside the enclosed GrowLab. If you must leave it outside, cover the reservoir to reduce evaporation.

    If you are using moisture grids in trays, fill the tray to the top of the grid with water.

2. **Completely cover your light garden with a plastic tent.** Sealing the unit in this way will prevent moisture from escaping, forming what amounts to a large terrarium. Make sure the covering is tucked inside the base. Otherwise, condensation will drip outside.

    Cover plants with plastic bags if you don't have a GrowLab or other light garden framework, or if you have large, rapidly growing plants that are in danger of using all of the moisture in their soil during vacation. Pull the bag over the plant and tuck the bag opening into the top of the pot. Moisture that condenses will run back into the pot, continuing to water the plant. Support the bag inside with sticks so the bag doesn't touch the leaves. Don't leave the plant in strong sunlight or it will scorch.

When covering your garden, be sure to attach the covering inside the frame on the side of the unit where electrical components are mounted. If you do not have a framework for your plant stand, do not drape anything directly over the light fixtures.

Prefabricated GrowLab fixtures are riveted, so must be returned to the manufacturer for repair. For assistance, call the National Gardening Association's customer service department: (800) 538-7476.

3. **Reduce the number of hours your lights are on.** Although fluorescent lights produce little heat, they do produce some, and the longer they're on, the more water the plants will use for growth. Plants can easily get by on ten hours of light each day for short periods.

4. **If you are using a heating cable, don't leave it plugged in.** The heat would speed evaporation of water from the base and pots. An exception to this is if there is a danger of temperatures dropping very low during vacation. Leave the cable on in these circumstances after checking with the custodian regarding safety precautions. (If you must leave a heating cable on, you'll need to find a reliable person to come in and water your plants every few days.)

5. **If you have someone come in to water your plants,** make sure the person is reliable, will come in once or twice a week, knows what to do, and will seal up the covering again afterward.

6. **When you return, uncover the plants and check carefully for signs of insect or disease problems.** These problems can develop easily in those still, warm, humid conditions. Check immediately so you can take action if necessary. If the soil and air are very damp after having been covered, remove the tent until they dry out a bit.

Chapter 5

Tackling Pests and Other Problems

A real advantage of indoor school gardening is that you can grow crops without having to protect them from most of their natural enemies. For instance, we don't find Mexican bean beetles, tomato hornworms, cucumber beetles, or woodchucks in our indoor gardens. Unfortunately some pests, and a number of diseases, can thrive in the warm, moist, predator-free environment that the indoor garden may provide. Don't be concerned that the appearance of pests and diseases will spell the end of your garden. Even insect-laden plants can produce a crop, and can certainly lend another dimension to your lessons! Armed with the information in this chapter, you and your students can address problems that do arise.

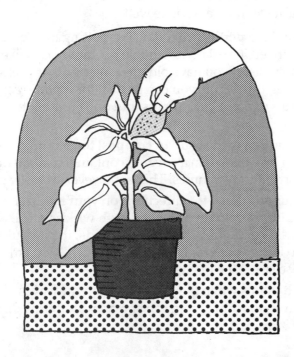

Prevention: The Best Medicine

The most important means of avoiding disease and pest problems is to prevent them from becoming established. This means being vigilant, providing conditions for healthy plants (healthy plants are the best defense against such problems), and practicing strict classroom garden hygiene as described below.

Pay attention. Ask the children to look carefully at their plants at least once a week. Take the pots out of the garden, lift them up, and get a good look at the soil and the underside of leaves. (This is a favorite spot for insects.) There are always students who love to be detectives in search of pest or disease clues. A magnifying glass can be a useful and exciting tool for this job.

Don't wait if you notice a problem developing. Take action immediately before the problem has a chance to become well-established and spread to other plants.

Don't bring in houseplants that could have diseases or insect problems. This will only invite trouble. If you must bring in house plants, reduce the risk by inspecting them carefully and by quarantining the newcomers in another part of the room for a few weeks.

Remove damaged, diseased, or weakened plant material regularly from the indoor garden. These materials attract insects and provide ripe conditions for diseases to develop.

Maintain good air circulation within the garden. Diseases can thrive in a stagnant environment, but will be less likely to do so if there is good air movement. Your students' daily movement around the classroom garden will provide some air circulation. If you're using a covered light garden, lift up the covering if conditions are too humid (see page 47). Don't overcrowd plants. Thin plants when they are young to ensure good air circulation.

Disinfect your equipment. Make a solution of ½ cup of chlorine bleach in 1 gallon of water. Use it to wash any pots you'll reuse. Rinse the pots in clear water to remove bleach residue. At the end of every year, replace the base material of your garden or clean it with a bleach solution, and rinse well.

Always use clean potting mix. Reusing potting mix, unless you have pasteurized it, will invite trouble. Commercial soilless mixes are already sterile. If you have old growing mix that was already used with healthy plants, you can reuse it for repotting houseplant cuttings or other large plants, but don't reuse it for young, fragile plants.

If you have added garden soil or compost to your mix, you can pasteurize it by baking it in a covered container in a 180-degree oven for thirty to forty minutes. This is, however, a smelly process.

Fertilize properly. Read the directions on your fertilizer carefully. Too much fertilizer can cause lush growth which will be weak and extremely susceptible to attack. (Aphids, in particular, are attracted to foliage with high levels of nitrogen.) Too little fertilizer can also stress the plants.

Don't touch plants when they're wet. When the leaves of your plants are wet, touching them can spread waterborne diseases.

Use good watering practices. Watering too often deprives the roots of air and promotes rotting. Not watering enough stresses the plants and makes them more susceptible to disease and insects. When you plant seeds, make sure your potting mix isn't so wet that you can wring water out of it, since algae and fungi will develop in the wet environment. When you water, avoid splashing or wetting the leaves for the same reason.

Environmental Problems

Even when you have used careful prevention techniques, pest or disease problems can develop. When you notice a problem, what should you do?

Sometimes symptoms that are misconstrued as signs of pest or disease problems may actually be the result of poor management or other problems. For instance, if your plants are stunted, yellowing, or otherwise abnormal looking, it may be from over- or underwatering or because container drainage holes are plugged up. Or, plants may be too close to the fluorescent lights, making the leaves dry and scorched.

Before dismissing plants as diseased, study Table 9, review information regarding plant needs and nutrient deficiencies and excesses, and try to assess the problem.

Table 9 indicates some possible environmental causes of common symptoms that your plants may exhibit. Similar symptoms can result from various causes. In determining the cause, consider the environmental conditions, location of the garden, and your own maintenance practices.

Pest Problems

If your class detectives do turn up evidence of pests in your garden, use the following information to help identify and control them. (See page 61 for detailed descriptions of the pest controls recommended here.)

Aphids—These are soft-bodied insects with both winged and non-winged varieties. Both types are quite visible, generally along the underside of leaves, on stems, and on flower buds. They may appear pale green, grey, white or tan.

Damage: When there is an infestation, leaves turn yellow and curl, and the plant will be generally weak. Aphids, like many insects, make a plant more susceptible to disease. They also transmit certain diseases.

Control: You can keep aphids in check with a soapy water spray. Although these treatments probably won't eliminate aphids from your plants entirely, they will reduce the population. You'll need to be constantly vigilant once aphids appear, so that you can notice reinfestation and respond quickly.

Whiteflies—These are very small (1/16 inch) white, winged insects found primarily on the undersides of leaves. When an infested plant is disturbed, these pests fly up in a cloud of white.

Aphid
1/10" Long

Whitefly
1/20"–1/12" Long

Damage: Whiteflies cause little direct damage to a plant, but their presence may lead to disease.

Control: Soapy water works the same way as with aphids but may be less effective since whiteflies can fly away and return when the treatment is complete. Spray every three to five days since the young develop rapidly. Since whiteflies are attracted to yellow, many people hang yellow boards covered with a sticky substance, such as 90 weight oil, to trap them.

Environmental Causes of Poor Plant Health — Table 9

Possible Causes	Foliage					Growth			Flowers		
	Wilted	All Leaves Dropped	Oldest Leaves Dropped	Yellowish Greens	Tips Brown	Plant Died	New Leaves, Small	Spindly, Weak, Thin	No Blooms	Pale Color	Buds Dropped
Insufficient Light (impairs photosynthesis and flowering)			●	●		●	●	●	●	●	●
High Temperature (especially at night, impairs growth and flowering)	●		●	●			●	●	●	●	●
Low Temperature	●					●					●
Overwatering or Poor Drainage (reduces soil aeration; roots die or nutrients can't be absorbed)	●	●	●	●	●	●	●	●		●	●
Lack of Water	●	●	●		●	●	●				●
Too Much Fertilizer (injures plant roots and becomes toxic to plant)	●	●	●	●	●	●	●				●
Lack of Fertilizer			●	●	●		●	●		●	●
Compacted or Heavy Soil (reduces root growth and activity)	●		●	●		●	●			●	●
Low Humidity, (a danger particularly in winter)	●		●		●						●
Fluorescent Light Scorch (plants too close to lights)				●	●						
Lack of Pollination											●

Mealybugs—These are soft-bodied, tan insects covered with white, cottony fluff. They may be found on the undersides of leaves and at joints of stems.

Damage: An infestation of mealybugs will weaken a plant and may lead to disease.

Control: Because of their waxy coating and tenacity, mealybugs can't be controlled well with soap and water. You can control them with a rubbing alcohol and water solution.

Spider Mites—These are tiny, oval, reddish, barely visible dust specks. You'll find them first on undersurfaces of leaves but they later spread to other parts. In heavy infestations, you'll see a silky webbing over the leaves.

Damage: An infestation causes stippling, bleaching, curling, and dropping of leaves.

Control: Periodically wash plants with a stream of water.

Soil Insects—There are a number of soil insects, including fungus gnats and springtails, that you may notice flying around your plants. They are most often a problem when you use garden soil or compost in a potting mix.

Damage: They are generally not harmful (although offspring can damage plant roots) but may indicate other problems. They thrive where humidity is high and where there is rotting organic matter around.

Control: Practicing strict garden hygiene and preventing excessive humidity are your best bets.

Rodents—Some teachers have experienced problems with small rodents in their gardens.

Control: Traps, set out of children's reach and with careful warnings, can be effective. If the problem is serious throughout the school, your principal and custodian should handle the problem professionally.

Pest Controls

We recommend soap spray and rubbing alcohol as the primary measures for controlling many indoor pests.

Soap Spray—These sprays are safe for use on food plants and are very effective in controlling a number of plant pests including aphids, whiteflies, and spider mites. Not all soaps are equally suited to this task. Some can be caustic to your plants and all can be harmful if used in too concentrated a solution. The best soaps to use are either gentle dishwashing soaps (not detergents), or commercial insecticidal soaps. Use as directed or dilute at the rate of 2 tablespoons per gallon of water.

Application: Spray the solution on the affected plants with a plant mister or small pressure sprayer, covering the foliage thoroughly. Make sure to spray under the leaves. You can also dip the entire plant in a container of the soap solution. If you are unsure about the effect of applying a particular soap, test it out on a small area of the plant and watch for results. Watch for signs of reinfestation and spray again in a few days, if necessary.

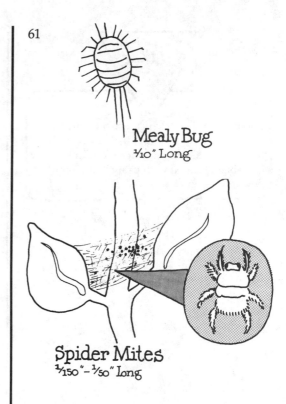

Mealy Bug
1/10" Long

Spider Mites
1/150"–1/50" Long

Soap Spray

Botanical and synthetic pesticides are toxic substances. We strongly discourage their use in the classroom. Indoor food crops that have been treated with pesticides should never be eaten.

Rubbing Alcohol
—Rubbing alcohol can control indoor pests such as mealybugs. However, it can damage plants if it is applied improperly.

Application: If the infestation is small, apply to pests one at a time using a cotton swab. If pests are too numerous to treat individually, mix a half-and-half solution of water and rubbing alcohol and spray the affected parts with a mister. Since alcohol may harm certain plants, rinse plants immediately after the treatment with clear water.

Homemade Pest Controls
—There are many homemade pest controls (garlic sprays, cayenne sprays, etc.) that gardeners have used with varying degrees of success. You can find recipes and suggestions for homemade insect controls in many gardening books.

Botanical and Synthetic Pesticides
—**We recommend the safest, most environmentally benign pest controls for your indoor garden.** Using such methods can become a part of important lessons in health and environmental stewardship. If an infestation gets out of control, and you feel as though you risk losing a substantial portion of your beloved garden, you may be tempted to use either a botanical (plant derived) or synthetic chemical pesticide.

We strongly discourage the use of botanical or synthetic pesticides in the classroom. These pesticides are not only persistent in the environment (botanicals much less so) and toxic to specific pests, but can also be toxic to beneficial insects and to humans.

Because they are toxic substances, many states restrict their application and their use around children. You, the teacher, may therefore be liable for misuse and for any problems associated with use of pesticides in the classroom. Before purchasing any of these substances, read the following precautions and contact your local county Cooperative Extension agent, principal, and superintendent for advice.

When using any pesticide, be sure to take the following precautions:

Identify the pests. It's important to know what pest you are trying to get rid of. Do you have a pest, or is it really a disease or environmental problem?

Read the label carefully and thoroughly for instructions on which insects it controls, how to apply it, and how to use and store it safely. The only way to apply a pesticide is according to the directions on the bottle.

Never use a substance that lists "danger-poison" or "warning" on the label. Such words on a label signify the level of hazard of the substance. (In decreasing order of toxicity these words used on pesticide labels are: "Danger-Poison," "Warning," and "Caution".) Pesticides that indicate "Caution" are the type most commonly found on the shelves in retail garden centers, and are the *only* ones that you should ever use.

Never eat indoor food crops that have been treated with pesticides. Although the label may list the number of days you need to wait between applying the pesticide and eating the crop (days to harvest), this applies only to outdoor crops since weather speeds the degradation of the poison.

Always take infected plants outdoors for treatment so students aren't exposed. Leave them outdoors as long as possible after application. Treat them just before a weekend or vacation to minimize exposure.

Store pesticides in their original containers in a locked cabinet or room out of the reach of children. Again, read the directions carefully for proper storage and container disposal procedures.

Dispose of pesticides properly. Most have a shelf life of at least two years, but remain a toxic waste. Don't dump them down the drain or put them in the trash. Contact your county Cooperative Extension Service agent or state Environmental Protection Agency for information on safe disposal of a particular product.

Dispose of empty pesticide containers properly. Don't reuse them for any purpose. Rinse thoroughly several times and use the rinse water as a last spray on your plants. (Don't dump it down the drain!) Wrap empty containers in several thicknesses of newspaper before putting them in the trash.

Diseases and Algae

The best way to avoid disease problems is to provide ideal conditions (good air circulation, watering, and fertilizing practices, etc.) for your indoor garden and to practice strict garden hygiene. It's difficult to eradicate diseases once they become established, so prevention pays off! If you think you may have disease problems, refer to the information below.

Powdery Mildew—This will primarily affect cucumbers, zinnias, and possibly beans in an indoor garden. Leaves will appear to be dusted with a white powder and will eventually turn brown and wither. The disease will weaken and finally kill the unsightly plant.

Control: Increase air circulation by uncovering the garden. Allow the garden to dry out between waterings.

Grey Mold—Plants affected with this disease develop brown patches that eventually become covered with grey or brown fuzzy mold. It is a mold commonly found on dead plant material in moist conditions and it can migrate to healthy plants.

Control: Clean up dead plant debris. There's no control for affected plants. Remove and discard all affected materials to prevent spreading.

Damping Off—This fungal disease causes seedlings to rot suddenly at the soil line and fall over. It may prevent seeds from germinating. It affects the seedlings of many vegetable and flower plants (see illustration).

Control: Prevent damping off by covering newly planted seeds with 1/8 inch of sphagnum peat moss. Remove and discard any affected plants and the soil around them. Discard or sterilize potting mix and containers in which affected plants were growing.

Bean Mosaic—This is a viral disease carried by aphids or by seeds of infected plants. It causes bean leaves to appear puckered, and eventually, to yellow and die. It weakens the plant and may interfere with fruiting.

Control: There is no control for viral diseases. Prevent them by keeping the aphid population down. Remove and discard affected plants immediately. (If you have only a few bean plants, you may want to keep them in order to observe the progress of the disease, since it won't affect other crops.)

Fungi and Algae—These appear as fuzzy white, dry brown, or green (algae) growths on the soil or base material surface. Although they're not real problems in themselves, they do indicate moist conditions and poor air circulation, which could lead to other problems.

Control: If you notice these growths, stir the soil or base material with a fork or your fingers once a week. Also, dry out the whole garden by uncovering it and increasing air circulation.

Algae will be more likely to form on your base material in the presence of intense fluorescent light. To avoid this, in a partially filled growing unit, cover exposed portions of the base material with aluminum foil, heavy cardboard, or dark plastic sheets.

note:

Do not confuse fungi and algae with the dry, crusty white buildup of fertilizer salts that may form on top of the soil if pots are not watered thoroughly. If you notice this dry, crusty buildup, loosen the soil with a fork and water thoroughly to flush out salts.

Chapter 6

Indoor Gardening Special Projects

Y ou can do much more than grow vegetables, flowers, and herbs from seed in your Grow Lab. Many teachers use their indoor gardens to start special projects that enhance plant science investigations and help expand on concepts such as vegetative propagation (growing new plants from parts of old plants), plant adaptations, and ecosystems.

Some of these projects also produce results such as houseplants, colorful bulbs, or thriving terrariums which can be sent home with students, sold at a special garden sale, or used to brighten the classroom.

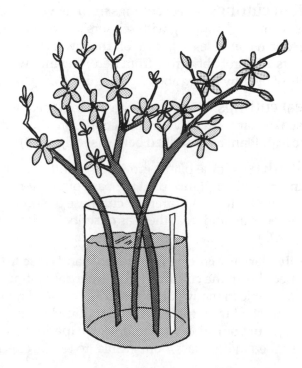

figure A

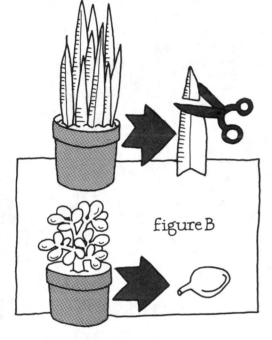

figure B

figure C

note:

Many people root cuttings in water. Although some plants will seem to develop nice roots with this method, the roots that develop have fewer root hairs, are more brittle, and often transplant poorly. Your class can conduct an experiment comparing the growth of cuttings rooted in water and other rooting mixes.

Houseplant Cuttings

Taking and rooting cuttings from plants is an easy way to increase your collection quickly, and to teach about vegetative propagation. Many common houseplants will root nicely in a light garden or on a windowsill. These new plants can be repotted and sent home with children, left to brighten the classroom, or sold at a plant sale. Below is a list of some common houseplants recommended for this purpose.

Stem Cuttings	Leaf Cuttings	Plantlets
impatiens	snake plant	aloe
coleus	jade plant	spider plant
chrysanthemum	begonia	piggyback plant
African violet	African violet	
geranium		
philodendron		
wandering jew		
Swedish ivy		

How To Root Cuttings

1. **Water plants well the day before taking cuttings.** This will prevent dehydration after cutting.

2. **You can root many cuttings in one container to save space and soilless mix.** Repot them once they've rooted. Use your soilless mix (or an equal volume mix of perlite and vermiculite) as a rooting medium. The mix should be moist, but not soaking wet, or your cuttings will rot.

3. **Fill the container with mix and make small holes** (½ inch to 1 inch deep) **with your finger or a pencil around the container.** The holes may be spaced as closely as 2 inches apart.

4. **Next, take cuttings as described below and be sure to hold them by the leaf, not by the stem.** If leaves are damaged, new ones can grow, but a damaged stem can kill the plant.

   Stem cuttings—Take cuttings from newer, faster growing stems, by snipping with scissors just below the third or fourth pair of leaves. Strip off the lower pair of leaves (roots will probably grow from here) leaving two to three sets of healthy leaves above (see figure A).

   Leaf cuttings—Cut a leaf with its stem (petiole) or, with a snake plant, cut a two-inch section from the middle of the leaf. Plant as described below (see figure B).

   Plantlets—Some plants grow tiny plantlets at the end of runners (spider plant), or at the base of the stem of the mother plant (aloe). Carefully cut these offshoots from the mother plant and treat them as described below (see figure C).

5. **Carefully place the cutting into the hole and close up the hole.** (Some people dip the cutting in a commercial rooting hormone, available in many garden centers, to speed rooting and prevent the stem from rotting. Using rooting hormone is not necessary, but your students can design experiments, like the one described in the Classroom Profile, to test its effectiveness.)

6. **Place individual containers inside plastic bags** and tie each one closed to retain moisture for rooting. Use plant labels to hold the plastic up and keep it from touching the leaves.

7. **Place the container under lights in a warm area.** A light garden offers a perfect environment for rooting. If you don't have a Grow Lab or other light setup, place containers in a warm, bright area, but avoid direct sunlight since the trapped heat could cook your cuttings.

8. **Check the containers occasionally to ensure that there is adequate water.** (There should be some droplets of water on the inside of the bag, but the bag should not be soaking.) If the soil appears too wet, punch a few holes in the plastic bag.

9. **To tell when plants have rooted, tug very gently on the cuttings.** Check after about two weeks and then at regular intervals. When you feel resistance, the cuttings are ready for transplanting. Gently lift them and transplant them into separate pots.

Bulbs

A bulb is a living "storehouse" that contains the embryonic stem, leaves, and flower of a plant. The bulb itself is a thickened underground stem that stores food for the growth of the plant. Bulbs have food reserves that enable them to grow and flower with no additional nutrients during the first year. Once a bulb flowers, the leaves must take in nutrients and photosynthesize in order to develop reserves to flower another year.

Bulbs that you can easily grow or force in the classroom include: crocuses, grape hyacinths, tulips, daffodils, and paperwhite narcissus.

How to Force Bulbs

1. **Purchase hardy bulbs for forcing in the fall.** This is when they are commonly available from garden centers and seed companies. If you won't be planting them right away, store bulbs in a cool (40 to 50 degrees), dry, dark spot. Because bulbs are living things, you shouldn't leave them unplanted for long. Try to plant the bulbs by the end of October.

2. **Plant bulbs in 6-inch pots filled with moist soilless mix** (three bulbs per pot). Bury the bulbs to their tips, with pointed ends facing up. (No fertilizer is needed since they have their own food stored within.)

3. **Place bulbs in a cold place** (garage, cold frame, or refrigerator) **for a minimum of eight weeks.** Since these bulbs are generally planted outdoors in the fall for a spring bloom, this cold treatment will simulate the winter conditions necessary for the formation of roots.

4. **Next, move the containers inside and put them under normal classroom light for two weeks.** Then put them under your indoor garden lights or onto a windowsill. They should bloom in two to four weeks. Once they have begun blooming, remove them from the bright lights of the indoor garden to encourage a longer bloom period.

Stimulating Rooting

A fifth-grade class, curious to find out which techniques might hasten the process of rooting in houseplant cuttings, set up an experiment to test various rooting methods. These methods included: dipping the cuttings in a commercial rooting hormone, providing bottom heat to the cuttings, feeding the cuttings with a fertilizer high in phosphorus, and even playing music for some cuttings! They compared the results of these trials with one another and with the control group and measured the total length of roots for each treatment after three weeks.

The paperwhite narcissus is the one bulb recommended here that doesn't require a chilling period. Plant these bulbs directly into your soilless mix from October until April. (If you store them until spring, keep them cool to prevent sprouting.) They should set roots, grow leaves, and flower in just six weeks in your classroom.

Growing Garlic

Garlic is another type of bulb that you can start indoors. Plant separate cloves with the flatter end down, 2 inches deep in soilless mix. Allow 3 inches between cloves. Garlic doesn't like too much moisture. It does best when you allow the soil to dry thoroughly between waterings. Almost any type of lighting (Grow Lab, windowsill, fluorescent light) will be adequate for garlic.

Have children crush and smell some of the leaves and describe the characteristic smell. The bulbs will form underground and will be ready to harvest after the tops yellow, in three or four months. Use the garlic as an ingredient in your garden salad dressing or experiment with garlic juice as a pest remedy!

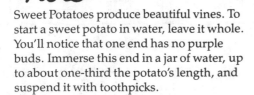

Sweet Potatoes produce beautiful vines. To start a sweet potato in water, leave it whole. You'll notice that one end has no purple buds. Immerse this end in a jar of water, up to about one-third the potato's length, and suspend it with toothpicks.

5. **If you want to try saving your bulbs for another year,** you must leave the foliage on after the blossoms have faded and fertilize the plants regularly. It's during this time that a bulb produces and stores food for next year's flower. Rather than attempting to force the bulbs the following year, you can plant them outside. It will still be two to three years before they'll produce another good bloom.

Tubers

A tuber is another type of underground stem that acts as a food storage organ. Tubers don't contain embryonic leaves and flowers as bulbs do. But tubers can be used to grow new plants. The most familiar example of a tuber is the potato. The surface of a potato has "eyes" that are actually buds. New potato plants are propagated by planting pieces of the tuber that contain eyes. (Explain to the children that this is exactly how farmers plant their potatoes.)

Sometimes potatoes are treated with a chemical to discourage sprouting, so start several, or buy certified "seed potatoes" from a garden center.

How to Grow a Potato Plant

Potatoes may either be started in growing mix or in water (to view root development). In either case, cut a white potato so that there is at least one eye in every piece.

1. **Starting potatoes in potting mix:** Place each piece in a 6-inch pot so that its top is about ¾ inch below the surface. Then set the pot in the classroom garden or on a windowsill. Although you won't be able to grow potatoes to maturity in such small containers, children will be able to observe early development of the plants.
(If you could grow potatoes to maturity indoors, you would find that the new tubers develop above the old ones and are attached by smaller stems to the main plant.)

2. **Starting potatoes in water:** Suspend a piece with eyes in water with toothpicks. Make sure to keep the eyes above the surface of the water. (The class can design an experiment comparing the growth of potato plants in water and in potting mix.)

A Mini-Orchard

Growing plants from leftover fruit seeds is an old classroom favorite. Although these plants will not mature into fruit-bearing trees, many do make nice houseplants. Fruit trees that grow in cooler climates (apple, pear, etc.) require a long chilling period before they sprout, so tropical fruit seeds may be a better choice for a class project. Adventurous gardeners might like to experiment with both.

The following tropical fruit seeds will produce lovely plants for the classroom: avocado, orange, lemon, lime, tangerine.

How To Grow an Avocado Plant

An avocado seed may either be started in water (to view root development) or in soilless mix. Your students can design an experiment comparing these two growing methods.

1. **Starting the Seed in Water:** Suspend the seed, pointed end up, two-thirds of the way into a jar of water, with toothpicks as supports. Germination will take about thirty days. Once the plant has a few leaves, transplant it into a pot of soilless mix.

2. **Starting the Seed in Potting Mix:** Fill a 4-inch pot halfway with moistened soilless mix. Put the seed, pointed end up, in the pot and fill the pot with mix to within ¾ inch of the top of the seed. Place it under lights or on a windowsill and keep it watered.

How To Grow a Citrus Plant

1. Soak seeds in water for twenty-four hours after removing from fruit.

2. Fill a 4- or 6-inch pot with moist soilless mix and plant the seeds ½ inch deep.

3. Keep seeds moist while they germinate. They should germinate in about a month and will grow nicely under fluorescent lights or on a windowsill.

4. Pinch the top shoots back when the plants reach about 12 inches tall, to encourage bushiness.

How To Grow a Cool Climate Fruit Plant

1. Chill cool climate seeds like apple and pear by planting them in moist sand or peat moss. Plant seeds about ½ inch deep in pots or flats.

2. Place the containers in a cold garage or a refrigerator for three months.

3. Plant into permanent pots as described under How To Grow a Citrus Plant.

Other Trees and Shrubs From Seeds

Collecting tree and shrub seeds from the wild to plant in the classroom garden can be a rewarding activity. Collect tree and shrub seeds as they mature, just before or after they drop from the tree in late summer or fall. If they cannot be treated within a day or two, store them in plastic bags in the refrigerator and treat them as soon as possible. If the fruits have a fleshy pulp that sticks to the seeds, wash them off before continuing.

In order to increase your chances of successfully germinating wild seeds, you need to understand a bit about dormancy. Many tree and shrub seeds are naturally dispersed in the late summer or autumn. If they were to germinate at that point, the plant might have to survive unfavorable winter conditions. In order to prevent

DIGGING DEEPER

Forcing Branches

You can clip the branches of many spring flowering shrubs and trees and bring them in the classroom to provide fragrant spring flowers. Timing is important when forcing branches. Cut them as described below, six weeks before they would normally bloom in your area.

Cut a 12- to 24-inch section of branch that has many plump flower buds (these are fatter than the leaf buds). Scrape with a knife or scissors along a 3-inch length of bark at the bottom of the cutting and place in lukewarm water for a day. Then move the cutting to a container of cool water and leave it in indirect light in the classroom. Change the water and cut an inch off the stem each week. Misting the branch several times a week will simulate spring rains and keep the buds full. You should have blossoms in three to six weeks. Move the cuttings to a sunny location once the buds open, for good color.

Branches for Easy Forcing

pussy willow – cut in late January
azalea – cut in February
flowering dogwood – cut in February
apple – cut in March
forsythia – cut in February

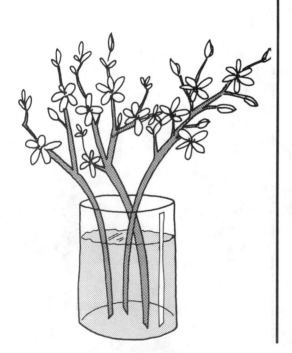

this from happening, many plants have developed control mechanisms that prevent the seeds from germinating until conditions are favorable.

One of the common forms of dormancy is caused by a hard seed coat which prevents water being taken up by the seed. Another common form of dormancy in the seeds of temperate climate plants inhibits the development of the embryo until it has been subjected to cold winter temperatures. You and the children can create conditions in the indoor garden to break the dormancy of tree and shrub seeds collected from the outdoors.

How To Break Seed Dormancy

1. Place the seeds in moist peat moss. Place the mixture in a plastic bag. If the seeds have hard coats (see list below), use a hard object to scar or chip a small part of the seedcoat away, or rub the seeds over a nail file or sandpaper.

2. Leave the seeds in a warm spot for three days. This will allow them to take up water and swell.

3. Then place the bag in a refrigerator for eight weeks.

4. Finally, remove the seeds. Plant them as described on the previous page.

The following list identifies seeds that are easy to germinate indoors if you follow the appropriate steps. In nature, there is great variation between different trees and conditions under which their seeds germinate, so don't expect to have consistent results. Try different types of tree and shrub seedlings including those not listed here. You can also design experiments to see how different treatments affect seeds.

barberry	maple	*redbud
crab apple	oak	Russian olive
*honeysuckle	pine	sweet gum
*magnolia		

*These seeds have hard seed coats and require scarring.

Terrariums

A terrarium is a miniature garden/landscape grown inside a covered glass or plastic container. It is an excellent tool for teaching children about the water cycle. Since it is an enclosed environment, the original water evaporates, condenses back, evaporates, and repeats the cycle. Some teachers have children create individual terrariums, while others prefer a collaborative class project.

How To Build a Terrarium

1. **Find an appropriate container.** Glass jars, fish bowls and tanks, plastic shoe boxes, etc., can all make fine terrariums. Many teachers make terrariums by cutting off the tops of large, clear plastic soda bottles, leaving a container that is 8 inches tall.

2. **Clean the container well and cover the bottom with ½ inch of sand or gravel to improve drainage.** Then fill to one-third full with woodland soil, garden soil, or potting mix. The soil should

be moist enough to cling together in balls when pressed into the hand. If you can find it, add a few granules of the kind of charcoal sold in gardening stores (don't use barbecue charcoal unless you're sure that it doesn't contain additives). This will help filter out impurities and keep the soil in good condition in this enclosed system.

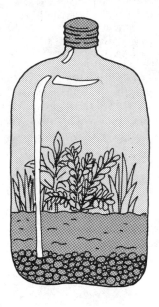

3. **Make small holes in the soil with your fingers to insert various plants.** Plants that can be used include:

> rooted cuttings of ivy, begonia, coleus, spider plant, asparagus fern, peperomia
> mosses from outdoors
> small flowering plants, tree seedlings, bits of bark, ferns, seeds (acorns) from the woods
> venus fly traps
> mimosa seeds (These are available through some seed catalogs. They germinate quickly and look like miniature trees.)

Be creative and experiment with different seeds, plants, and objects (rocks, bark, etc.) to make a diverse mini-landscape. If something doesn't thrive, remove and replant.

4. **Water the plants well and cover the container with plastic or glass.**

5. **Place the terrarium in your indoor garden or in a well-lighted classroom location.** Do not place it in direct sunlight or plants will scorch.

You'll know that the terrarium contains the right amount of water if the sides and top get misty with water droplets when in bright light. If there is no moisture along the sides, you should add some water. If the sides are always very wet, there's too much water, and you should punch holes in the top or remove it for a few hours to let some water evaporate. If you achieve the perfect balance, you may not need to water again. Check the moisture periodically, to be sure.

6. **If you used soilless mix, you'll need to fertilize as described on page 49.** If you have used rich woodland soil, garden soil, or potting mix with soil, you will not have to fertilize your terrariums. In fact, feeding would cause the plants to grow too large for their environment!

Chapter 7

Equipment Care and Maintenance

Proper care and maintenance can extend the life of your indoor gardening equipment. This chapter identifies and addresses technical problems and details proper cleaning and storage procedures. Since there are some differences between the pre-fabricated and build-your-own models, pre-fabricated GrowLabs come with their own complete assembly instructions. Please note that pre-fabricated GrowLabs do not include a ground fault circuit interrupter.

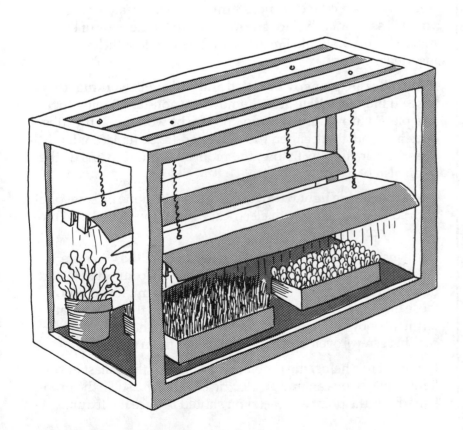

Troubleshooting

The Grow Lab is designed to be as trouble-free as possible so that teachers can concentrate on teaching. However, sometimes equipment does malfunction. The following simple tips will help you identify the problem and decide how to solve it. If you feel uneasy about diagnosing problems, consult with your custodian. Be sure to also read Appendix D for details on the Grow Lab electrical components.

Problem: None of your light fixtures work
Possible Solutions: First check to make sure that your main plug is plugged into a functioning wall outlet. Check the outlet by plugging in something you know to be in working order.

Check to see that your timer is operating (see below).

Check your ground fault circuit interruptor (see below).

If you have checked all of the above and none of your lights are working, you should consult an electrician for assistance. The problem must be in the main cord or outlet box.

Problem: Lights come on but are dim or flickering
Possible Solutions: Wait until the rooms heat up. Temperatures below 45 degrees Fahrenheit may affect light operation.

Make sure that the tubes are properly installed. A loose tube can cause flickering or total failure of *both* tubes in the fixture. This kind of problem is the source of most lighting failures.

At both ends of each light there are terminals (usually made of plastic), and the tubes are installed between them. In each terminal is a slot into which the pins on the tube are inserted. After the tube is inserted in both terminals, twist it a quarter turn until it is seated correctly and is firm. When it is seated correctly, you will see a small bump, groove, or mark at the ends of the tube. This mark should line up with the slot into which you inserted the pins.

If the tubes are properly installed and still aren't working, check to see if they are still usable. Remove the non-functioning tube and place it in a fixture that you know to be working. If the tube does not work there either, the tube needs to be replaced. If it does work in the new fixture, the problem is probably inside the original light fixture.

Check inside the light fixture. This should be done by someone with some experience with electrical wiring. You can take off most covers by removing screws or clips.

Once inside, look for loose wires. Check where the wires are inserted into the terminals and where they are connected to each other and to the power cord. Gently tug on them. If you find a loose one, try to reconnect it by pushing it into the appropriate terminal or by reconnecting it in the wire nut (that little conical cap that screws over wire ends and makes them connect.)

If none of this helps, the problem may be with the ballast in your light. Unless you can find an electrician who will solve the problem, this is the point at which you should replace the fixture.

Caution

Always turn off or unplug lights before adjusting tubes or removing light covers.

Problem: Your timer isn't working (but electricity is on).

Possible Solutions: Thoroughly read the directions that came with the timer. Check to see that the timer setting pieces are in the correct place and that the timer is properly set.

Check the override switch on the timer.

Make sure that your lights are plugged into the timer outlet. If they are not plugged directly into the timer (or into a multi-outlet strip connected to the timer), it will seem as though your timer is not working.

If it is not working at all, check the ground fault circuit interruptor.

Problem: Ground fault circuit interruptor (GFCI) not working or constantly tripping.

Possible Solutions: If the timer is no longer humming, check the GFCI to see if it has been tripped off. If the "T" button is pushed in, leaving a red bar showing on the "R" button, the GFCI has been tripped for some reason. Press the reset button to resume power. (If there is a real electrical problem, the GFCI will trip off again for safety. Chances are, however, the unit will resume operation.)

If the GFCI trips frequently, make sure the plastic in your Grow Lab does not enclose the ground fault circuit interruptor. These are very sensitive devices that may be tripped off by humidity. Lift part of the plastic to allow for increased air circulation.

If the timer continues to trip, check all wire connections and look for frays. A short circuit is probably occurring.

Problem: Heating cable isn't working

Possible Solutions: Check the plug connection to see if it is properly attached. This is particularly important if you installed a plug from a kit.

Check to see if the heating cable is broken. This generally happens when they are not well secured to the base of the growing unit. The heating cable crosses itself, the resulting heat melts the insulation and causes the cable to short and break. Close examination of the cable will reveal this condition. *Never* use a damaged heating cable. A heating cable cannot be repaired. Replace it or give it up entirely since it's not critical to the operation of the classroom garden unless your building is extremely cold for extended periods.

GFCI

Cleaning and Storing Equipment

It pays to take care of your classroom garden at the end of the school year, whether it will be spending the summer in your classroom, stored away in a supply closet, or transported back to some central location. Proper care can help to avoid summer damage, loss, or theft. Cleaning and storing your Grow Lab, as described below, should ensure that it remains safe and sound over the summer months, and that it will be complete and ready for action come fall.

Take extra care when using bleach solution around children.

1. **Discard all used soil mix (composting it, if possible), and clean pots and trays with a solution of ½ cup bleach to 1 gallon of water.**

2. **Remove the perlite, capillary mat, or moisture grids from the base of the unit.** If you have perlite and would rather save it than purchase new material next year, you can clean it. Soak it in the same bleach solution for an hour. Then rinse it well in clear water and spread it out on sheets of plastic to air dry for two days. When completely dry, store it in a trash bag or covered container. Wash capillary matting or moisture grids thoroughly in a solution of ½ cup bleach per gallon of warm sudsy water. Rinse them well and leave them out to dry before storing.

3. **Clean the base of a homemade indoor garden using the same proportion of bleach solution.** Clean the aluminum frame of a prefabricated GrowLab with soap and water. Be sure to dry the frame well before storing it. If you have plastic in the base, check for holes, repair them with duct tape, then store the plastic.

4. **Unplug the lights and clean the fluorescent tubes.** Wipe the tubes with a damp cloth. (You'll want to do this again before you reinstall lights in the fall, since dust can significantly cut down on the light that reaches your plants.) Reinsert the tubes into the fixtures or wrap tubes individually in several thicknesses of newspaper and store them in a safe place. Wide-spectrum or full-spectrum bulbs will retain their useful life for two to three years under normal use. Cool white bulbs should be replaced annually.

5. **Take down the light fixtures if they are on chains.** Wrap up their cords. Place the fixtures tube side up in the base of the GrowLab to protect them from breakage during moving.

6. **Unplug the timer, and store it out of sight in a bag or box.**

7. **Cover the whole GrowLab with paper or plastic to keep out dust.**

Chapter 8

Sharing the Excitement and Building Support

As with any new school program or piece of equipment, your Grow Lab and indoor gardening activities are sure to arouse the curiosity of students, other teachers, administrators, parents, and members of the community at large. Many will want to know what you're up to. Some will want to help or start a garden of their own. A few will question the educational value of your program, or have safety or other concerns about it.

Anticipate people's natural curiosity. Plan to inform and involve them. Below you'll find ideas from other indoor gardening teachers on ways to share the excitement and build ongoing support for your gardening program.

Involving Your Whole School

Leave your door open! Everyone loves to see living things thriving and sprouting, particularly during the winter when they're aching for a touch of spring.

Share the harvest. Invite the principal, superintendent, other students, and teachers to your salad feast! Raise flower seedlings to brighten the schoolyard.

Publish information about your gardening program in a school newsletter. Invite other classes in for a tour and talk conducted by your students.

Give the school board a presentation on your program. Explain how it enhances the curriculum.

Present garden-related curriculum units at a staff meeting. Show your fellow teachers how they can start gardens in their classrooms. Lead inservice workshops for your colleagues. Here you can inform other professionals about your gardening program, trade ideas with other gardeners, and enrich your own knowledge. Inservice topics might include:

> Indoor Gardening – How to Get Started
> Science Experiments in Your Gardening Laboratory
> Teaching Nutrition with Your Indoor Garden
> Houseplant Propagation
> Art Activities for Indoor Gardeners
> Fundraising with Your Classroom Garden
> Interdisciplinary Studies with a Gardening Focus

Involving Parents

An indoor gardening project is a great way to get parents involved in your classroom. Have children write letters to their parents, explaining the project and encouraging them to visit and participate. Some teachers hold Grow Lab open-house days or evenings during which children give presentations on the school garden. A weekly or monthly class newsletter that outlines garden-related curriculum units and updates readers on plant growth keeps parents informed. Some parents who garden will be thrilled and flattered at an invitation to talk to the class or lead an indoor gardening activity. It's always helpful to have an extra pair of adult hands, especially on planting days. In some schools, parents have donated plants and other materials. Parents or parent organizations might partially finance or donate labor to build a Grow Lab for your class or for another teacher.

Involving Community Volunteers

Your school gardening program can attract a variety of volunteers —experts, willing to come to diagnose a specific garden problem, or to share their own particular gardening interests. Perhaps someone will lead a special garden activity or workshop with your students. Others may help conduct teacher inservice workshops.

In some districts, experienced gardeners have been offered the

Your local Cooperative Extension office offers a wealth of free or low-cost printed technical information as well as personal assistance. Local 4-H programs (the youth component of Cooperative Extension) often work with schools on gardening programs. Consult your county office to find out how to use its resources and to find out about other horticultural resources in your area. To find the number for your local office, look under *Cooperative Extension, Extension,* or the name of your county in the phone book.

chance to take teacher inservice workshops on indoor gardening in exchange for their volunteering to visit classrooms later in the year. In this way, they can learn the new skills of indoor gardening and, in turn, use their own gardening experience to help in the classroom.

You might find volunteers through:

    local garden clubs
    botanical gardens
    parent organizations
    Master Gardeners' program or 4-H program of your local
        county Cooperative Extension Service

Encouraging Media Coverage

Indoor school gardens can really capture the attention of the media. Tell a feature editor where he or she can get pictures of smiling children and ripe tomatoes growing in February and you'll find a photographer at your door in no time.

Media coverage can boost spirits and camaraderie and help ensure that hands-on, garden-based education will find a place in more and more classrooms throughout the country.

Indoor school gardens lend themselves to special events, ranging from harvest fairs to salad parties and plant sales. And special events lend themselves to media coverage. Don't be put off if reporters don't cover your best show. Sometimes other news takes precedence, but keep trying and you'll get results.

Don't forget about local radio and television stations that have gardening shows, or that might appreciate the opportunity to do a good human interest piece. Garden editors of major newspapers might well be interested in such a story—and what a thrill for the kids!

Provide the superintendent of schools with information on your project for reports or mention at a regular press conference.

Once you do have a news article or coverage in the media, be sure to thank the appropriate people for the story, and keep them informed as your program develops. Then use it! Display it proudly in the classroom and circulate copies to your principal and school board. Use the publicity in rounding up support and money you need.

Seeking Financial Support

Once you have built, rented, or purchased an indoor garden laboratory, you will have yearly needs for replacing supplies such as pots, potting mix, and fertilizer. Many teachers have discovered ways to obtain these supplies without making great demands on tight budgets.

Seek donations or discounts for supplies. Some teachers have their students write letters or make presentations to managers of garden supply stores. (This is a practical lesson in the power of clear communication!) When you or your students solicit donations, be sure to explain the objectives of your school gardening

project clearly. Describe how the donation will be recognized. Many classes have found that garden center managers offer both enthusiastic support and sound gardening advice.

Other organizations to approach for donations of new and used gardening materials include:

> botanical gardens
> local garden clubs
> university or city greenhouses
> local service clubs
> community garden groups

Local garden clubs, botanical gardens, service clubs, and foundations sometimes sponsor or "adopt" indoor gardening projects. Support has included funding the purchase, rental, or building of a Grow Lab and sponsorship of district-wide school gardening programs. These partnerships between the classroom and community groups can have more than just financial benefits, as students and the group members share information, exchange letters, and develop friendships.

Thanking Supporters

Saying thanks is important. If people know their gift was appreciated and well-used, they are more likely to continue giving. Encourage your students to take on this task. Heartfelt thank-you letters, drawings from the children, and photographs of abundant indoor gardens surrounded by smiling faces, are among the most valued ways of saying "thanks" to supporters.

In many schools where outside organizations have donated, built, or financed Grow Labs, each Lab carries a small plaque, visible to all who visit, that lists and thanks the supporters.

If you have received donations from individuals, local groups, organizations, or businesses, include them in your thanks. Give your supporters prominent mention in any newsletter, information package to parents, media story, news conference, harvest fair, etc. Be sure to thank parents and others who have volunteered their time or expertise.

Appendix A

Indoor Garden Growers' Guide

The classroom garden Growers' Guide is a general reference that provides information on growing and harvesting vegetables, flowers, and herbs in your classroom. This guide suggests specific, well-suited varieties. If you follow the guidelines in the Growers' Guide table, the growing and harvest information, and the management information in the main text, you should be rewarded with a successful garden.

This general guide, however, contains a limited amount of information. There is more information available on specific plant needs, varieties, etc. We encourage you to use this guide as a springboard. Read through other gardening references and experiment on your own with new crops, varieties, and growing techniques.

Growing and Harvesting Vegetables

Remember that certain crops like corn and potatoes, and heading crops, such as cabbage, cauliflower, and head lettuce, will not grow properly to maturity indoors. But any crops that transplant well can be started early in a light garden, or on a sunny windowsill, and transplanted later outdoors. (See page 24 for a list of crops that transplant well.)

Beans—Choose bush beans over pole beans, since most will grow only to 18 inches and will remain compact enough to benefit from the fluorescent lights. (If you are gardening on the windowsill, try growing pole beans and training them to climb up strings by the windows.) **Harvest:** Beans should be harvested when the pods are full but before the outline of the enclosed seed shows. Pick pods when they are mature, to encourage growth of younger pods which will mature over several weeks.

Beets—Beets are easy to grow indoors, but they may not measure up to garden beets with regard to size. Roots are likely to be small and slow-growing. **Harvest:** Beet greens, which are rich in vitamins, are best harvested and eaten when young. They are delicious cooked or raw in salads. Leave some greens to continue supplying food to the roots. The roots, which you can feel under the soil with your fingers, should be harvested when they are just over 1 inch in diameter.

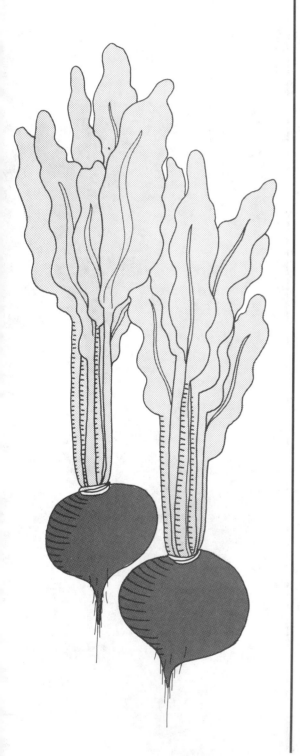

Carrots—Carrots, like beets, are easy to grow indoors but grow rather slowly. The most helpful thing you can do for your carrots is to thin them properly, since crowding will prevent the growth of good roots. If the carrot shoulders push above the soil, cover them with soil to prevent the exposed parts from becoming dry and green. **Harvest:** Pull carrots when they are ¼ to ½ inch in diameter.

Chinese Cabbage (Bok Choy)—This is a nonheading type of Chinese cabbage with a thick, celerylike midrib and tender leaves, which are edible raw in salads or cooked. It will grow to about 16 inches. **Harvest:** Pick young leaves to eat raw and take second cuttings and older leaves for cooking.

Collards—Collards have coarse, cabbage-like leaves. Unlike other members of that family (cabbage, broccoli, and cauliflower), collard plants do not form heads, so they will perform well under lights. You can use the young greens in salads and older greens for cooking. **Harvest:** Pick young leaves for eating raw and older leaves for cooking. If you pick just the leaves and leave the stem, the main stem should produce another crop.

Cucumbers—Male flowers will appear first and will greatly outnumber the female flowers. Once you have some of both, hand-pollinate them as described on page 53. When choosing seed, look for compact, bush-type varieties. Be aware, however, that even these types can take up a lot of space.

Eggplant—These warm weather plants prefer soil depths, but will produce in containers indoors. Look for dwarf varieties when buying seed. There are also a number of specialty varieties such as long oriental and white types. **Harvest:** Pick fruits when they are dark purple and glossy.

Lettuce—The looseleaf varieties grow best under lights. Heading types won't form heads indoors. Lettuce prefers cool temperatures and plenty of water. Keep it moist to prevent it from becoming bitter. **Harvest:** Harvest outer leaves as needed or cut the plants at soil level for a larger harvest. If you leave the roots in the soil and keep fertilizing and watering them, they will produce another crop in about eight weeks. If lettuce is left growing for too long, particularly with hot temperatures, it will become bitter.

Mustard Greens—This is a beautiful, vitamin-rich, green, leafy plant. Its appearance contrasts nicely with many of the other indoor garden crops and its sharp flavor will be a novelty for some students. **Harvest:** Harvest leaves 4 inches or smaller for salad, and larger if you plan to cook them. If you leave a short piece of stem when cutting leaves, you will get another harvest in about four weeks.

Onion Tops—An advantage of growing onions is that all parts can be used at any time in their life cycle. We do not recommend growing onions to mature bulbs in the indoor garden because this takes so long. (Bunching onions, sold for scallions, also have a long growing season and we don't recommend them.) Instead, plant regular onion varieties from seeds or sets and harvest them as greens. Onion seeds generally do not remain viable for more than a year, so make sure that you're starting with fresh seed each season. **Harvest:** Snip tops during the young, tender green stage.

Parsley—This is a slow-growing crop, but it can produce a reasonable harvest in a single pot. Once sprouted, it is relatively trouble-free and can continue producing throughout the year. Soak seeds overnight in water before planting to facilitate germination. **Harvest:** Harvest sprigs as needed. As long as some foliage is left, the plant will continue to produce more leaves.

Peanuts—Although these may take up to five months to mature indoors under lights, they are beautiful plants and can be an exciting addition to the indoor garden. A couple of months after planting, bright orange/yellow, pea-like flowers will form. The small flowers that form lower on the plant are the ones that will be fertile. After self-fertilizing, they will bend downward and bury themselves. Add soil to the top of the pot to help bury them. **Harvest:** Look periodically at the developing peanut under the surface. When mature, the kernels will look plump and will have the distinctive peanut texture with pronounced veins. If left too long, some varieties will resprout and begin to grow new plants from the young peanut. Shell them and toast the raw seeds in a pan, while stirring, over low heat, for ten to fifteen minutes. Sprinkle with salt and enjoy!

Peas—Although many of the garden varieties of peas are quite tall, there are a number of shorter varieties that you can raise under fluorescent lights. Peas require cool conditions. Growth will slow considerably when temperatures exceed 60 degrees. Unless your room is very hot, however, you should be able to get a small, token harvest indoors. **Harvest:** Start picking when pods have swelled to an almost round shape. Don't let overmature pods stay on the plant; this will cut down on your yields.

Peppers—Although peppers are relatively slow to mature, they produce a nice crop of rather small fruits and provide an interesting addition to the indoor garden. They do require rather warm temperatures at blossom time in order to produce fruit, so if your room temperature does not stay between 65 and 80 degrees, we do not recommend that you grow them. Ornamental peppers, available in most seed catalogs and garden centers, are even slower to mature, but they make very nice gift plants. The tiny, colorful fruits are also edible and are very spicy. **Harvest:** Clip peppers from stems as soon as they reach usable size (2 inches in diameter). They can also be left on the plants to turn red or yellow

Radishes—Radishes give the quickest results of all indoor garden crops. They produce a large number of roots in a single pot, only four weeks from planting. Make sure to keep them well watered, thinned, and close to the lights, to promote good root development. **Harvest:** Harvest radishes when you see from the shoulders that they are the size of a small marble. They will become woody if they remain in the soil for too long.

Strawberries (Alpine)—These are small strawberries, grown from seed, that have a flavor reminiscent of wild strawberries. You can raise them as indoor plants or move them out to a garden or border. The seeds take quite a while to germinate, so make sure to keep them moist. **Harvest:** Harvest berries as they ripen. Plants will bear small fruits over a period of several months.

Swiss Chard—This is a good indoor crop since you can use it raw or cooked, like spinach. Unlike spinach, Swiss chard will grow well in the warm indoor environment of your garden. **Harvest:** Pick the outer leaves before they get tough, and new, younger leaves will grow from the center. If you want a continued harvest, don't pick all of the leaves.

Tomatoes—When buying tomato seed, look for designated container varieties. Tiny Tim is an old favorite of indoor gardeners because it is a vigorous dwarf tomato. It produces a profusion of nice-looking, small tomatoes in a relatively short time, and keeps producing for weeks. You can stimulate more fruit production by carefully pinching back the little shoots (suckers) that grow between the main stem and branches. Tomato plants may need to be staked or tied to the light garden frame for support. **Harvest:** If you want to hasten the ripening process, try placing a very ripe apple into a pot of green tomatoes. The ethylene gas produced by the ripening apple will stimulate reddening of the tomatoes. Although tomatoes will ripen off the vine, allowing them to ripen on the vine will provide best flavor and maximum production of vitamin C. Twist the fruit carefully from the stem when it's ready.

Turnips—You can easily grow turnips to a reasonable size indoors. These white-fleshed roots can be eaten either raw or cooked. Young turnip greens are very nutritious and, like beet greens, can be eaten raw or cooked. **Harvest:** Harvest as you would carrots, when the roots are between 1 and 2 inches in diameter.

Key To Planting Chart Headings (on following pages)

Suggested Varieties — We recommend these varieties because they perform well under indoor container conditions. You can use these or choose other varieties, keeping in mind such factors as number of weeks to maturity, special cultural requirements, and, most importantly, size and growth habits of the plant. You'll need to adjust the lights so they are close to all the plants in your garden so try to look for compact, low-growing varieties. You will find that there are miniature varieties of many vegetables and flower plants. Seed catalogs and packets often indicate which varieties are specifically suited for container growing.

Days to Germination — This will give you an approximate idea of when to expect your seeds to germinate, given reasonable conditions. Remember, room temperature, water, and a number of other factors can affect this rate.

Weeks to Maturity — Again, these are approximations of the number of weeks from planting until harvest.

Plants Per 6-Inch Pot — This is the pot size that we recommend. This column lists the number of plants that can be reasonably grown in each 6-inch diameter pot. Overcrowding pots will cause poor growth.

Plants Per Smaller Pot — Many teachers use small (3-or 4-inch pots) or ½-pint school milk cartons for planting, so we've included, for the vegetable crops, numbers of plants you can grow in these. Note: Some plants cannot be grown to maturity in such small pots.

Depth of Planting — Generally you should plant seeds at a depth three times their width. This column of the Growers' Guide lists specific planting depths. Some of the annual flower crops listed either require light to germinate or are too tiny to be buried under soil. A "0" appearing in this column indicates that the seeds should be planted on top of the soil and pressed down lightly with a smooth surface, but not buried.

Low Light — Many crops can be successfully grown on a windowsill or under only one or two light fixtures, but some will not produce well under these circumstances. To determine which crops will be more likely to thrive under lower light conditions, refer to this column.

Yield — Since the yields you can expect in an indoor garden are considerably less than you would expect outdoors, we have included, for many crops, a rough idea of the amount that you can expect to harvest from each 6-inch pot.

Nutrients Contained — This column includes information on vitamins and minerals provided in substantial amounts by each of the vegetables.

Vegetable Planting Chart

Crop	Varieties	Days to germi-nation	Weeks to maturity	Plants per 6" pot
BEANS	Contender Tendercrop	4-8	8-9	1-2
BEETS	Early Wonder Cylindra Mini-Ball Ruby Queen	5-12*	9-12	4-5
CARROTS	Little Finger Planet Kundula Short 'n Sweet Baby Finger Nantes	8-16	10-11	4-6
CHINESE CABBAGE (non-heading)	Pak Choy Crispy Choy	5-8	9-12	1
COLLARDS	Vates	4-6	11	1-2
CUCUMBERS	Bush Pickle Patio Pik Pot Luck Bush Whopper	5-10	9	1
EGGPLANT	Beauty Hybrid Dusky Japanese Long	20 +	12 +	1
LETTUCE	Tom Thumb Black Seeded Simpson Salad Bowl Prizehead Ruby Buttercrunch	4-8	7-8	4
MUSTARD GREENS	Green Wave Savanna	4-10	6-8	1-2
ONION TOPS	Southport Yellow Globe Southport Red Globe White Sweet Spanish	7-14	6-8	12 +
PARSLEY	Extra Curled Dwarf Italian (flat)	10-20*	8-10	4-6
PEANUTS	Early Spanish	7-14	20 +	1
PEAS	Little Marvel Laxton's Progress	5-10	8-10	1-2
PEPPERS	Yolo Wonder	8-14	9-12	1
RADISHES	Cherry Belle Early Scarlet Globe Sparkler French Breakfast	3-5	4-5	6-8
STRAWBERRIES (Alpine)		20	12 +	2
TOMATOES	Tiny Tim Patio Hybrid Pixie Hybrid Red Robin	6-10	10-12 +	1-2
TURNIPS	Purple White Top Globe Tokyo Cross	3-7	6-8	4
SWISS CHARD	Fordhook Giant	7-14	8-10	1-2

*These seeds should be soaked in water for 24 hours before planting.

Plants per smaller pot	Depth (inches)	Low light	Yield (approx.)	Nutrients contained
—	1-1½	No	6-10 per plant	protein, B, C
2	½	Yes	1"-1½" roots	greens high in A, C, iron, calcium
—	½	Yes	½" diameter, 2" long roots	A
—	½	Yes	2 cuttings	—
—	¼-½	Yes	2 cuttings	A, C, phosphorus, calcium
—	½-1	No	1-3 6" cukes per plant	—
—	¼-½	No	1-2 small fruits per plant	—
1-2	¼-½	Yes	4 small plants	A, potassium, calcium
1	¼-½	Yes	2 cuttings of 6" leaves	A, C, calcium, iron, B's
6+	½	Yes	continuous cuttings	potassium
1-2	¼-½	Yes	continuous cuttings	A,C
—	1½	No	3-6 per plant	protein, phosphorus, B's
—	2	No	4-6 pods per plant	protein, B_1, C, iron
—	¼-½	No	2 small fruits per plant	C, A
3	¼-½	Yes	½"-1" roots	C
1	1/8	Yes	4-8 tiny berries	C, iron
—	¼-½	Yes	6-15 small fruits per plant	potassium, A
1-2	¼-½	Yes	1"-2" roots	greens high in calcium, A, C, iron
—	½	Yes	continuous cuttings	A, iron, calcium

Growing Flowers

You can grow many annual outdoor garden flowers from seed to brighten the classroom. This section provides basic cultural information and suggested varieties. As with vegetables, when choosing varieties of annual flowers for indoors, look for relatively low-growing or dwarf types.

Ageratums—Because ageratums are low-growing flowers, nearly any variety will do. The flowers are compact, dense, woolly looking, blue, pink, or white puffballs.

Alyssum—Alyssum is another low-growing border plant that comes in a variety of cool colors including purples and white. Its delicate flowers take a while to bloom, but will bloom for a long time.

Coleus—This brightly colored plant is grown mainly for its attractive, variegated leaves. Although you can easily propagate coleus from stem cuttings, it can be fun to start these plants from seed. Press the tiny seeds into place on your growing medium and mist carefully. Pinch back the main stems to encourage branching and bushy growth. If you want to maintain the vibrant leaves, pinch off the small, blue flowers as they develop.

Impatiens—Impatiens are among the most difficult of these flowers to grow from seed, although you can grow them easily from cuttings. Their seeds are extremely small, and the seedlings are often susceptible to damping off. Nonetheless, their succulent stems and colorful flowers earn them a place on this list.

Marigolds—Dwarf marigolds are a great addition to the indoor garden. Once the seeds germinate, the plants grow well and produce a profusion of blossoms ranging from almost red to pale yellow. Pinch back the main stem to encourage branching.

Morning Glories—Although these plants twine and vine so much that they cannot actually be grown for long within a light garden, the trumpet-shaped, blue flowers add a nice accent to the gardening classroom when you grow them up strings near the window.

Nasturtiums—These plants serve a double purpose in your garden, producing brightly colored orange or yellow flowers and rounded leaves, all of which are edible. The lovely flowers and peppery-flavored leaves add a nice touch to garden salads.

Petunias—Petunia seeds are very fine and difficult to work with. Scatter them on top of soil mix and mist them until they germinate. These sturdy flowers will bloom for a long time in the classroom or outside.

Snapdragons—These colorful, dragonlike flowers can add a unique touch to the classroom garden. Choose dwarf varieties if growing under lights. If your flowers are sparse, your indoor garden may be too warm for their liking.

Zinnias—Zinnias can be the bright stars of your indoor garden. A dwarf mix will yield a wide range of colors over an extensive growing season. Seeds are larger and easier to handle than those of the other flowers listed here. The main problem with zinnias is their susceptibility to fungus problems.

There are many other garden annuals that may be brought to flower in the indoor garden, including those listed below. We encourage you to experiment.

asters (Gem mix)
begonias (fibrous dwarf)
celosia (Kewpie)
dianthus (Snowfire)
geraniums (Diamond)

phlox
portulaca (Afternoon Delight)
primula
salvia
verbena

You may find that certain plants produce lovely foliage and even buds, but fail to flower. This *may* have to do with the fact that some plants are short-day plants, meaning that they prefer to flower when they receive about ten hours of daylight. Since you will be leaving the lights in your garden on for fourteen to sixteen hours, some flowers may be hesitant to bloom under these conditions. Another reason for failure to bloom may be that they prefer blooming under cool conditions and your environment may be too warm.

Perennials —There are many types of perennial flowers which you can easily start in an indoor garden. They may be transplanted outdoors the following year. You might have children bring in dried seeds of various wild or cultivated perennials and experiment to see if you can germinate and grow them. Some of the easiest perennials to grow include: black-eyed Susan, Shasta daisy, coral bells, baby's breath, lupine, poppy, and foxglove.

Flower Planting Chart

Crop	Variety	Days to Germination	Weeks to Maturity	Plants Per 6" Pot	Depth* (Inches)
Ageratum	Blue Mink Blue Jeans	5-10	9	4-6	0
Alyssum	Royal Carpet Carpet of Snow	5-14	10-12	6-8	0
Coleus	Rainbow	10-14	—	4-6	0
Dianthus	Snowfire	10-14	9	4-6	1/8
Impatiens	Blitz Elfin	10-20	9	4-6	0
Marigold	Petite Mix Inca Gold	5-7	11	4-6	1/8
Morning Glory	Heavenly Blue	5-7	6-8	3-4	1/4
Nasturtium	Dwarf Jewel	7-14	8-10	1-2	1/2
Petunia		10	10-12	3-4	0
Snapdragon	Floral Carpet	10-15	10	3-4	1/8
Zinnia	Thumbelina	5-7	10	4-6	1/8

*Some of the flower seeds listed either require light to germinate or are too tiny to be buried under soil. A "0" appearing in this column indicates that you should plant these seeds on top of the soil, pressing down lightly on them with a smooth surface, but not burying them.

Growing Herbs

Herbs can add a fragrant dimension to the indoor garden. In addition to their culinary uses, many can be used for crafts projects such as wreaths, flavored vinegars, sachets, etc. You can use herbs at all stages of their lives and you can grow them either under lights or on a windowsill. However, herbs grow slowly compared to vegetables.

You can start all of the herbs listed in the Herb Planting Chart from seed, or from plants purchased at a nursery. Most herbs can also be started from divisions of adult plants (the exceptions to this are basil, coriander, dill, and summer savory, which are annuals). When purchasing seed, look for designated dwarf or mini-varieties.

Although many of the herbs will grow quite large if left to their own devices, you can regulate their growth and encourage bushiness by pinching back (and using) new top growth periodically. You should also pinch back developing flower buds to extend the usable life of the plant.

Herb Planting Chart

Herb	Days to Germination	Plants Per 6-inch Pot	Depth of Planting (inches)
Basil (annual)	7-10	2-3	1/8
Catnip	5-14	3-4	1/8
Coriander (annual)	10-12	3	1/2
Chives	5-14	20-30	1/4
Dill (annual)	5-10	3-4	1/4
Marjoram	10-16	2-4	1/8
Spearmint	10-16	3-4	1/8
Oregano	8-14	2-4	1/8
Parsley (see page 85)			
Sage	14-21	3-4	1/4
Summer Savory (annual)	14-21	1-2	1/2
Thyme	20-30	4-6	1/8

note:

Some of the herbs listed above as perennial may be annual, depending on the area of the country and the variety of herb.

Appendix B

Reproducible Worksheets

The National Gardening Association and the Knox Parks Foundation grant permission and encourage teachers to copy, for use with the Grow Lab program, the following worksheets.

Plant Journal

Plant Growth Chart

A Trip Inside A Bean Seed

The Life of a Bean Plant

Flower Power

Keeping a Plant Journal

As you watch your plant grow, pay close attention to its progress. Notice how it changes in response to your care. Start a journal like the one below.

THINGS TO OBSERVE AND RECORD:

- How the seeds sprout
- When you water
- When you fertilize
- Changes in the plant as it grows
- Number of leaves
- Color and shape of leaves

- Number of flowers
- Height of the plant
- Movement of the plant
- Signs of pests and diseases
- Taste (if it's edible)
- Experimental treatments

To keep track of your plant's progress, start a diary like the one below.

Date and Time	Notes	Drawing
Sept. 9 9:30 am.	This morning my plant has no new leaves. It is nice and green. The plant is bending toward the sun. I am going to turn it around so the sun shines on the other side. The soil is a little dry. I will add ½ cup of water.	
Sept. 10 10:30 am.	My plant is starting to straighten up. It's 15 inches tall today. A pair of new leaves is starting to form. The soil is still wet so I won't water it today.	
Sept. 11 9:45 am.	My plant is bending toward the sun today!	

Name _____

Date and Time	Notes	Drawing

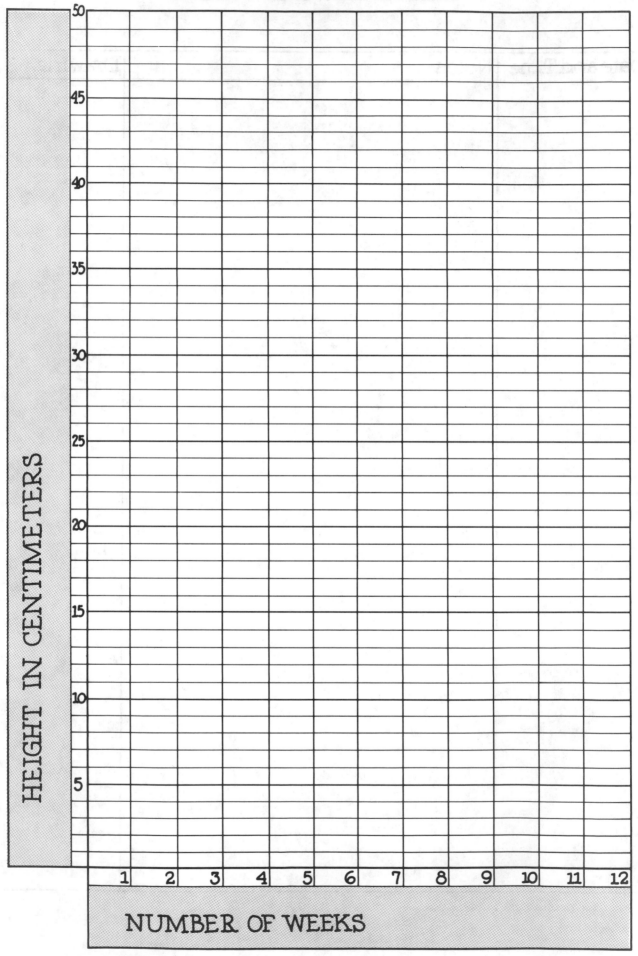

PLANT GROWTH CHART

HEIGHT IN CENTIMETERS

50

45

40

35

30

25

20

15

10

5

1 2 3 4 5 6 7 8 9 10 11 12

NUMBER OF WEEKS

A TRIP INSIDE A BEAN SEED

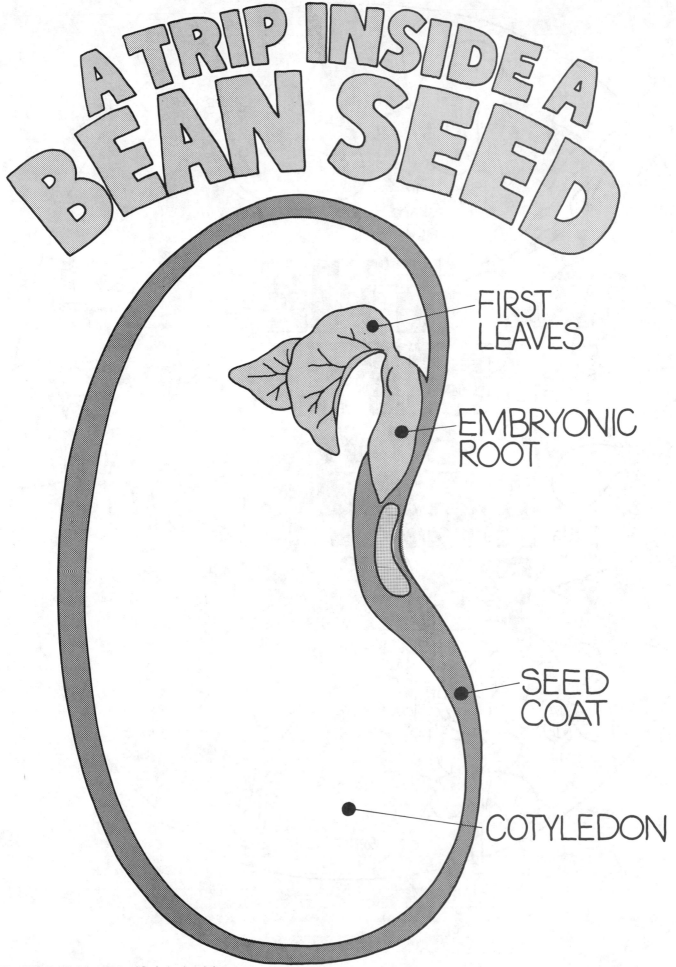

FIRST LEAVES

EMBRYONIC ROOT

SEED COAT

COTYLEDON

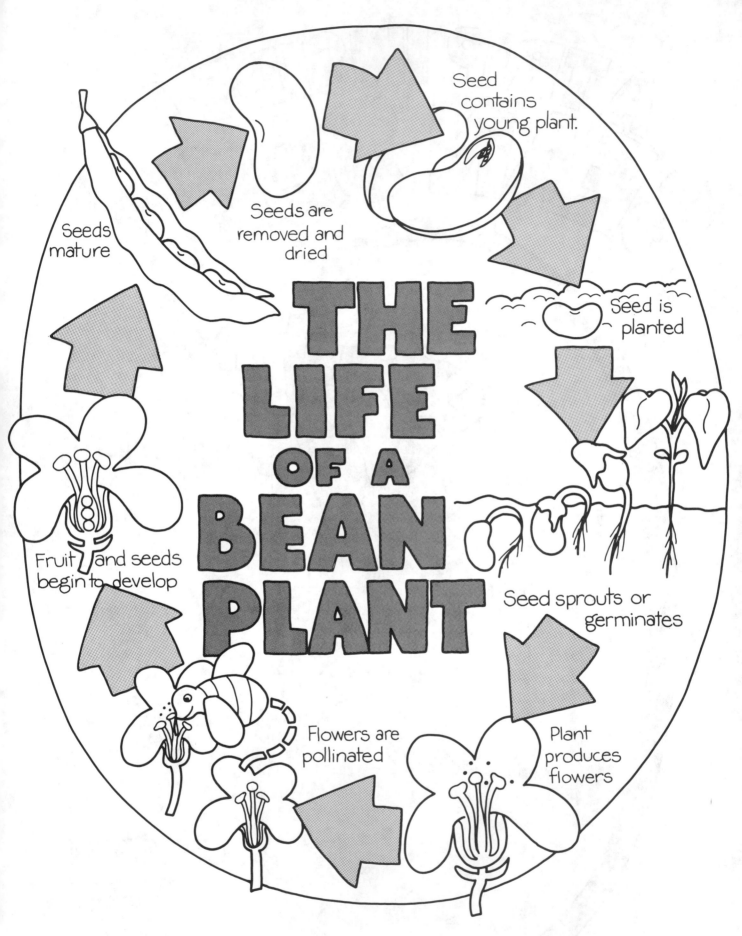

THE LIFE OF A BEAN PLANT

Seed contains young plant.

Seeds are removed and dried

Seeds mature

Seed is planted

Fruit and seeds begin to develop

Seed sprouts or germinates

Flowers are pollinated

Plant produces flowers

FLOWER POWER

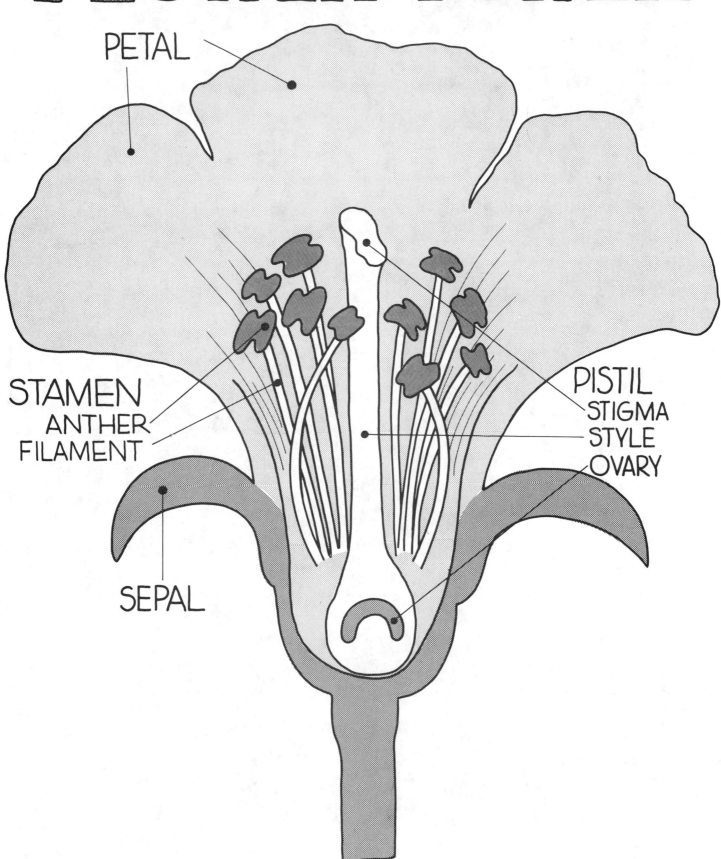

PETAL

STAMEN
ANTHER
FILAMENT

SEPAL

PISTIL
STIGMA
STYLE
OVARY

Appendix C

Supplies

Construction Plans for a Build-It-Yourself Grow Lab (Appendix D), provides information on purchasing supplies and electric components for assembling the basic Grow Lab Indoor Garden. This section has similar information for the supplies that you may need to purchase every year, and for supplies, such as light tubes and capillary matting, that you may need to purchase initially or replace periodically.

If there are a number of gardening classrooms within your school or school system, consider purchasing supplies in bulk to save money. Many greenhouse and nursery supply catalogs carry supplies such as pots, soilless mix, and fertilizer in bulk quantities. Several of these suppliers are listed in Appendix E.

Capillary Matting — Capillary matting is sometimes hard to find in retail stores. Check with local garden or greenhouse supply centers or purchase it from the National Gardening Association.

Fertilizer — Retail garden centers and discount stores carry a wide range of fertilizers, as do many seed, greenhouse, and nursery supply catalogs. Two to eight ounces of water-soluble fertilizer should be plenty for one year of classroom gardening, depending on your growing area.

Fluorescent Tubes — The best source for cool white and warm white tubes is your school custodian. Otherwise, your best source will probably be a hardware or discount store. Wide-spectrum tubes are available from the National Gardening Association.

Growers' Trays and Moisture Grids — Any plastic trays without drainage holes that are at least 2 inches deep and that fit inside your garden will be adequate water reservoirs. You can buy rigid plastic growers' trays for the base of your indoor garden through some of the catalogs listed in Appendix E. You can purchase sturdy Perma-Nest™ trays and moisture grid inserts through the National Gardening Association.

note:

Your GrowLab project will not require *all* of the supplies described here. See page 101 for a sample list of a year's supplies.

Perlite — Coarse perlite is most inexpensively purchased in 4-cubic-foot quantities from a greenhouse supply company or a large garden center, since it is used as an ingredient in potting mixes. This is enough for the 2-by-4-foot bases of three GrowLabs. Use 1 to 1½ cubic feet of perlite in each GrowLab.

Plastic Covering — You can purchase 4- or 6-mil polyethylene in 4-foot widths for covering and lining your indoor garden at many discount or hardware stores. Greenhouse supply catalogs also carry this plastic in very large quantities. Don't use lighter-weight plastic; it tears easily.

Pots — You'll readily find these at local garden centers and discount stores. You can generally get a good discount by explaining your project to a garden center owner. Since pots are more expensive retail, you may want to buy in bulk (100 or more) from a nursery or greenhouse supplier. Your students' parents may have an accumulation of pots at their homes they'd be willing to donate.

Potting Labels — These wooden or plastic 4- to 6-inch potting labels are like popsicle sticks. You can purchase them either in large quantities from greenhouse supply catalogs or in smaller batches through seed catalogs, or even craft stores. Similar sticks are often ordered for elementary school art programs.

Seeds — Many classroom gardening teachers seek donations of seeds from local garden centers or seed companies near the end of the summer, when many companies want to get rid of excess stock. See Appendix E for a partial list of mail-order seed suppliers.

Soilless Mix — Retail packages of soilless mixes at discount stores and garden centers tend to be very small and expensive. Local garden supply centers often carry large 4- to 6-cubic-foot bales, one of which will be enough to last three seasons in the average gardening classroom. Try to locate soilless mixes locally, as the mail-order price of shipping such a heavy item is quite high.

Waterproof Marking Pens — These are valuable for marking labels, since the labels will certainly get wet. Laundry markers will do, but they are often thickly tipped. Garden centers and many seed companies offer fine-tipped waterproof pens. Pencils, although harder to read, are adequate for writing on labels.

note:

Starter kits in two different sizes, containing pots, plastic labels, specialty seeds, soilless mix, fertilizer, insecticidal soap, and a watering can can be purchased from the National Gardening Association.

Sample Cost of a Year's Supplies for a Homemade GrowLab

Costs of supplies for an indoor garden will vary with the supplier, with the geographic region, and over time. The following sample list outlines the cost of consumable supplies for the first year. Keep in mind that some of the materials, such as plastic pots, will not necessarily need to be replaced yearly.

perlite	16 qt. (if used as base material)	6.00
soilless mix	1 cu. ft. compressed bale; makes 45 qt.	9.00
fertilizer	8 oz. water soluble	4.00
pots	25 6-inch and 30 4-inch pots	15.00
seeds	10 packets @ 1.50 each	15.00
wooden or plastic pot labels	50 @ .06	3.00
plastic (for sides and base)		5.00
marking pen		2.00
	Total:	$59.00

Electrical Costs

The cost of electricity for operating lights and a timer will vary with electrical rates. Based on a price for electricity of 9 cents per kilowatt hour, the price of running three fixtures (six tubes) will be approximately $10 per month.

Appendix D

Build Your Own Grow Lab™

These plans are divided into two sections: 1) Constructing the Wooden Frame and 2) Assembling Electrical Components. Before beginning this project, read through these instructions and study the diagrams in order to understand the scope of the project. This will help as you collect the proper tools and materials. Once you have the materials and tools you need, assembly of the Grow Lab will take from seven to fifteen hours, depending on your level of expertise.

The National Gardening Association's Grow Lab construction plans have been reviewed by licensed electricians and expert carpenters. This unit is known to be safe, sturdy, and effective. The parts listed are easy to find and the procedures are straightforward. You may already have some of the materials and can save money by substituting your own or using recycled materials if they are in good condition.

note:

Before beginning, make a photocopy of the three template patterns on the following page. You will follow the instructions on the templates to mark drill holes for your rails and cross supports.

Constructing the Wooden Frame

You can purchase all of the materials for the wooden frame at a building supply store or lumber yard. The board dimensions and hardware are all standard sizes so that you can build the Grow Lab with a minimum of tools. If you have access to a table saw, you can save money by cutting other pieces of new or recycled wood to size.

Using top quality clear grade softwood (such as pine or fir) for the frame will improve the finished appearance and make the assembly of your Grow Lab easier. However, #2 grade lumber will cut your costs considerably and is an acceptable substitution. If you choose the cheaper grade, try to get lengths that are straight and have few knots.

Frame Materials

- (5) 1″ x 4″ x 10′ clear or #2 grade lumber (actual dimensions ¾″ x 3½″ x 10′)
- (2) 2″ x 2″ x 8′ clear or #2 grade lumber (actual dimensions 1½″ x 1½″ x 8′)
- (1) 48″ x 24″ x ⅜″ CDX plywood (bought pre-cut or cut from a 4′ x 8′ sheet)
- (16) 3 x ¼-20 slotted head bolts with nuts
- (32) ¼″ (inside diameter), ¾″ (outside diameter) flat washers
- (1 lb.) 1¼″ drywall screws
- (4) ¾″ drywall screws
- (1) quart white exterior latex paint and brush
- (1) small can wood filler, latex caulk or Bondo (optional)
- (5) sheets 100 or 120 grit sandpaper

Tools Required

crosscut hand saw or electric circular saw
carpenter's square
tape measure
electric drill
⁵⁄₁₆″ and ⅛″ drill bits
#1 Phillips screwdriver bit or Phillips screwdriver
adjustable wrench
slotted screwdriver

Template Patterns

(instructions on following page)

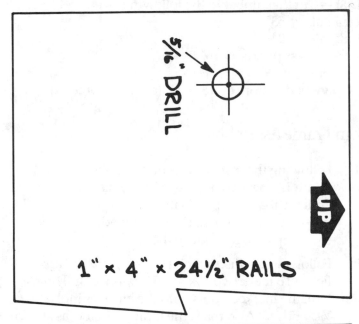

5/16" DRILL

UP

1" × 4" × 24½" RAILS

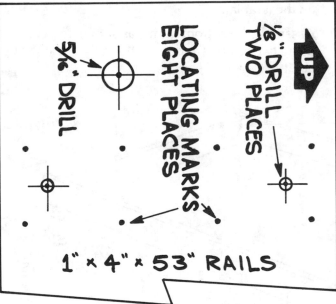

5/16" DRILL

⅛" DRILL TWO PLACES

UP

LOCATING MARKS EIGHT PLACES

1" × 4" × 53" RAILS

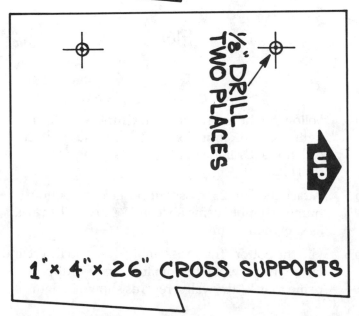

⅛" DRILL TWO PLACES

UP

1" × 4" × 26" CROSS SUPPORTS

Template Patterns Directions

FIG. 1A

1. Align template with left end of board and using a sharp pencil, mark through the pattern to locate the drill hole.
2. Flip the pattern over so that this face is down; align on the right end of the board and mark.

FIG. 1B

1. Align template with left end of board and using a sharp pencil, mark through the pattern for the three drill holes and the eight locating marks.
2. Flip the pattern over so that this face is down; align on right end of board and mark.

FIG. 1C

1. Align template with left end of board and using a sharp pencil, mark through the pattern to locate the drill holes.
2. Flip the pattern over so that this face is down; align on the right end of the board and mark.

Assembling the Frame

1. **Cut List**—Cut the lumber to the following sizes:
   - (4) 1 x 4 rails @ 53"
   - (4) 1 x 4 rails @ 24½"
   - (6) 1 x 4 cross supports @ 26"
   - (4) 2 x 2 posts @ 39"
   - (1) ⅜" plywood bottom @ 48" x 24" (cut if not pre-cut)

2. **Bottom Frame Assembly**

   Step 1. Following the instructions on template pattern figure 1A mark two 1" x 4" x 24½" rails for drill holes. Drill the marked spots with a ⁵⁄₁₆" drill bit. (Note: To preserve the template patterns for additional use, use a copier to reproduce them.)

   Step 2. Following the instructions on template pattern figure 1B mark two 1" x 4" x 53" rails for drill holes. Drill the marked spots with the bit sizes indicated: ⁵⁄₁₆" and ⅛". Also mark the locating marks as shown on the template.

   Step 3. Assemble the bottom frame, as shown in figure 2, using two 53" rails and two 24½" rails. Fasten with eight 1¼" drywall screws.

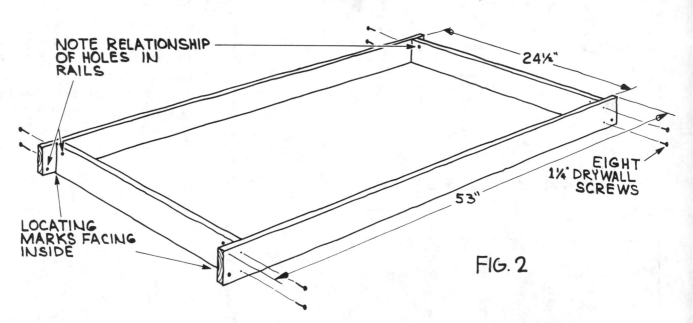

FIG. 2

   Step 4. Following the instructions on template pattern figure 1C mark four 1" x 4" x 26" cross supports for drill holes. Drill the marked spots using a ⅛" drill bit.

   Step 5. Attach the four 26" cross supports to the bottom frame assembly using sixteen 1¼" drywall screws as shown in figure 3.

   Step 6. Flip the bottom frame assembly over and insert and fasten the plywood bottom to the cross supports using four ¾" drywall screws as shown in figure 4.

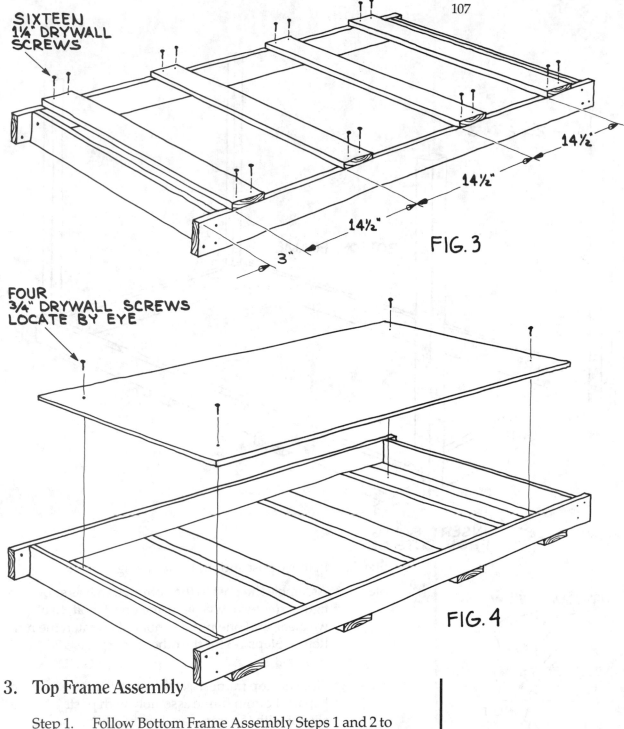

**SIXTEEN
1¼" DRYWALL
SCREWS**

14½"

14½"

14½"

3"

FIG. 3

**FOUR
¾" DRYWALL SCREWS
LOCATE BY EYE**

FIG. 4

3. Top Frame Assembly

Step 1.   Follow Bottom Frame Assembly Steps 1 and 2 to mark and drill remaining rails using template patterns 1A and 1B.

Step 2.   Assemble the top frame (same as bottom frame as shown in figure 2) using two 53" rails and two 24½" rails, and fasten with eight 1¼" drywall screws.

4. Attaching Top Frame To Bottom Frame

Step 1.   Set a 2" x 2" x 39" post in position against the bottom frame as shown in figure 5. Through the two predrilled holes in the frame corner rails, mark the post for drill holes with a pencil or appropriate size punch.

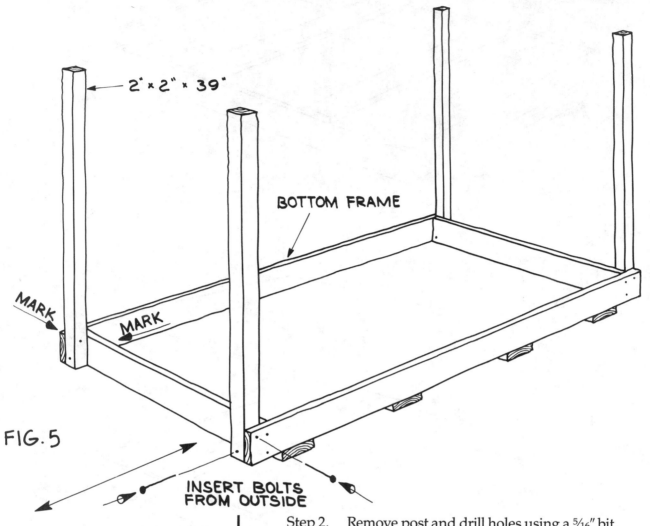

2" x 2" x 39"

BOTTOM FRAME

MARK

MARK

FIG. 5

INSERT BOLTS
FROM OUTSIDE

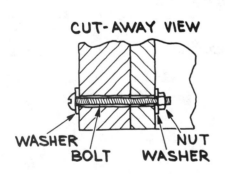

CUT-AWAY VIEW

WASHER
BOLT
NUT
WASHER

Step 2. Remove post and drill holes using a 5/16" bit.

Step 3. Assemble the post to the bottom frame as shown in figure 5 (cut-away view) using one 3" bolt, two washers, and one nut. Do not fully tighten the nut. Repeat Steps 1-3 for the other three posts and corners.

Step 4. Place the top frame assembly on a flat work surface. Flip the bottom frame assembly with posts over and align it with top frame as shown in figure 6. Use a pencil to mark each post for drill holes through the two pre-drilled holes in the frame corners, as done in Step 1. Mark the remaining three posts.

Step 5. Remove bottom frame assembly with four posts and place upright. Drill marked holes in posts using a 5/16" bit.

Step 6. Place bottom frame assembly with posts back into top frame assembly as in Step 4 and assemble one post to the top frame assembly using one 3" bolt, two washers, and a nut as in Step 3 (figure 5). Repeat for other posts.

Step 7. Using an adjustable wrench, tighten all sixteen nuts on bottom and top assembly and flip unit upright.

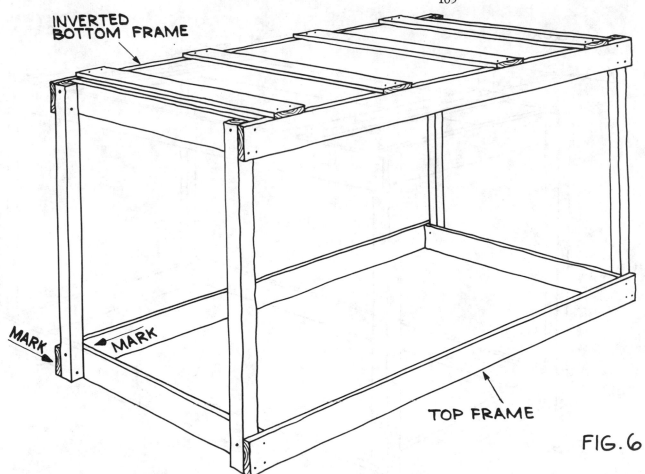

INVERTED BOTTOM FRAME

MARK

MARK

TOP FRAME

FIG. 6

5. Mounting Top Light Supports

Step 1. Following instructions in template pattern figure 1C, mark two 1″ x 4″ x 26″ cross supports for drill holes. Drill the marked spots with a ⅛″ drill bit.

Step 2. Measure the distance between the two existing holes on fluorescent fixture used for hanging the fixture, as shown in figure 7.

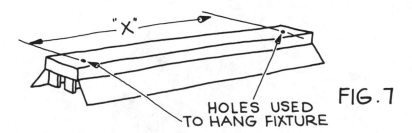

"X"

HOLES USED TO HANG FIXTURE

FIG. 7

Step 3. Use this dimension as the approximate center-to-center measurement to locate the two remaining 26″ cross supports on top of top frame, as shown in figure 7A. Fasten with eight 1¼″ drywall screws.

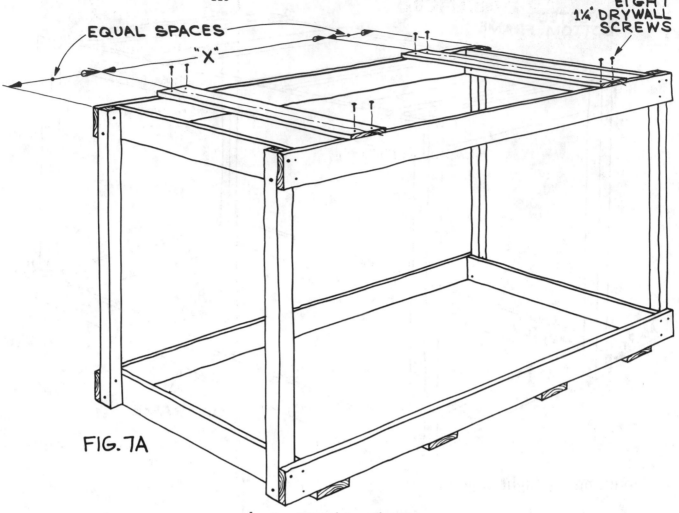

EQUAL SPACES

"X"

EIGHT
1¼" DRYWALL
SCREWS

FIG. 7A

6. Finishing the Frame

Step 1. Fill all holes and defects with wood putty; sand rough spots.

Step 2. Paint using two coats of white exterior latex paint.

Assembling Electrical Components

Tools Required

sharp knife
slotted screwdriver
Phillips screwdriver or electric drill with #1 Phillips bit
heavy duty wire cutter
wire stripper
needle nose pliers

Electrical Materials

(3) UL-listed 48" two-tube fluorescent light fixtures. (See important information on page 112 regarding purchasing fixtures.) Fixtures must be able to be opened to access ballast for rewiring of cord.

The following materials list and instructions assume you will be rewiring 3 light fixtures.

(1) UL-listed residential grade ground fault circuit interrupter receptacle (GFCI) and cover plate.
(20') 16/3 copper electrical cord. (You can use heavier wire, #14 or #12, but do not use smaller wire, which has a gauge number higher than 16.)
(4) Three-prong electric plug and cap.
(1) Metal 2" x 4" surface-mounted electrical outlet box.
(1) UL listed surface mounted multi-outlet (4-6 outlets) receptacle strip with grounded plug cord.
(4) ½" Romex connector collar.
(9) Small wire nuts. (Note: wire nuts may come with light fixtures.)
(4) ¾" drywall screws.
(6) Eye hooks.
(12) S-hooks. (Note: 2 S-hooks may come with each light fixture.)
(18) Feet of #3 chain.
(1) 20' self-regulating heating cable (optional).
(1) 28" x 54" sheet of 6 mil plastic.

All wiring must be carried out by, or under the supervision of, an adult experienced with electrical wiring.

note:

You won't need to rewire light fixtures if you can find UL-listed light fixtures with an extra-long power cord (36" from the end of the fixture or 60" from the center of the fixture. However, it is normally very difficult to find such fixtures. This extra length is required to allow for height adjustment of light fixtures. If you have these fixtures you may eliminate three Romex connectors, ten feet of 16/3 copper electrical cable, three electric plugs (three prong), and all wire nuts from your materials list.

You can also avoid wiring fixtures if you can locate the type of 2-foot, 12-gauge, grounded, UL-listed, three-outlet adapter illustrated below. In this case, you can use light fixtures with short cords and may eliminate the materials described above as well as the multi-outlet receptacle and Steps 1-5 under Installing Lights.

Instead of rewiring light fixtures, plug the short cords on your fixtures directly into the three-outlet adapter. Plug the other end of the adapter plug directly into your grounded timer.

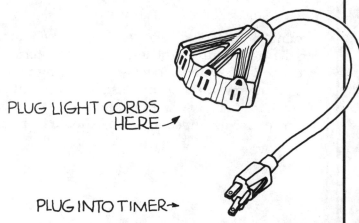

PLUG LIGHT CORDS HERE ➤

PLUG INTO TIMER ➤

Use only receptacles, plugs, and electrical devices that are grounded.

Purchasing Electrical Supplies

You can purchase most electrical supplies at well-stocked lumber and building, hardware, or department stores. Industrial-grade light fixtures and grounded timers can be purchased at electrical supply stores or through the National Gardening Association.

Fluorescent Fixtures — There are various types of fluorescent light fixtures that may be used in a GrowLab. Shop lights, which cost between $10 and $15, are the type you will probably find at discount or hardware stores. They have metal side reflectors that reflect light onto plants and help prevent tube breakage. Shop lights are often built with a low-quality ballast, which may decrease the life expectancy of the fixture.

Higher-grade light fixtures with heavy-duty ballasts are available at electrical supply stores or through the National Gardening Association for $30 to $40. The ballasts on these higher grade fixtures last longer and make less noise than shop lights. Look for fixtures with metal side reflectors and at least 4 inches between bulbs to provide better light distribution to plants.

Heating Cable — If your GrowLab will reside in a room that seems too cool to promote good plant growth (see page 46), you can install a heating cable beneath the base material. (See lighting and electrical wiring assembly procedures for information on installing your heating cable.)

A self-regulating, three-watt heating cable requires no thermostat. This type of heating cable can be purchased at hardware stores by the foot along with a do-it-yourself end cap and plug.

Heating cables with built-in thermostats are available at many garden centers. These are often referred to as soil heating cables. Care must be taken in installing and using this type of cable, as it can burn out if misused.

Ground-Fault Circuit Interrupter — A ground-fault circuit interrupter (GFCI) protects you against hazardous electrical shock that may be caused if your body becomes a path through which electricity travels to reach ground. If there is a short circuit, the GFCI will cut off quickly enough to avoid electrical injury.

Ground faults should be tested every three months by pushing the "test" button. The test creates an internal short circuit to check if the system works. If functioning properly, the "reset" button will pop out. Push the reset button back to its normal position. If it does not move, the ground-fault circuit interrupter is not functioning and should be replaced.

Wiring Electrical Controls

1. Mounting Electrical Outlet Boxes

Step 1. Fasten the 2" x 4" electrical box and the multi-outlet strip receptacle to the left top rail, using four ¾" drywall screws, as shown in figure 8.

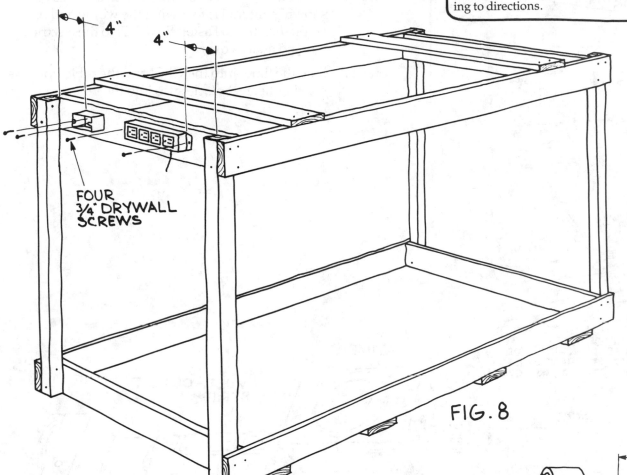

4"

4"

FOUR
¾" DRYWALL
SCREWS

FIG. 8

2. Wiring Power Supply (power cable, plug, GFCI)

Step 1. Cut one piece of 16/3 electrical cable 10' long. Use a knife to remove 1" of outer insulation from one end, making sure not to cut the insulation of the three inner wires. Use the wire strippers to remove ½" of insulation from each of the three inner wires, as shown in figure 9.

Step 2. Attach each of the three inner wires to the appropriate screw of a three-prong plug, as shown in figure 9. Tighten the three internal screws, the two strain relief screws and reattach the fiber cover.

1"

½"

FIBER
COVER

GROUNDED
PLUG

POWER
CORD

WHITE WIRE TO SILVER SCREW
BLACK WIRE TO BRONZE SCREW
GREEN WIRE TO GREEN SCREW

FIG. 9

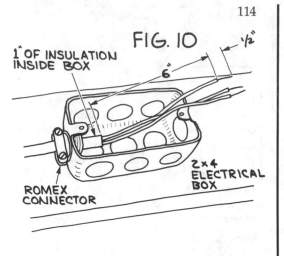

FIG. 10

1" OF INSULATION INSIDE BOX

6"

½"

ROMEX CONNECTOR

2 x 4 ELECTRICAL BOX

Step 3. Remove from the opposite end of the 10' piece of cable, 4" of outer insulation and ½" of insulation from the ends of the three inner wires, as shown in figure 10, following the same procedures as Step 1.

Step 4. Remove a circular "knock-out" from the electrical box and install a Romex connector in the box as shown in figure 10. Insert stripped end of the cable through the connector into the box so that 1" of unstripped cable is inside the box as shown in figure 10. Tighten the two screws on the Romex connector.

Step 5. Install the ground fault circuit interrupter as shown in figure 11, following the wiring and orientation directions. Fasten the GFCI to the electrical box and attach cover.

Step 6. Plug the timer into the GFCI and the cable from the multi-outlet receptacle strip into the timer as shown in figure 12.

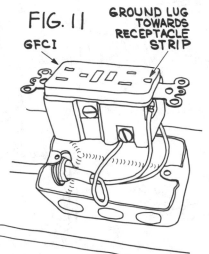

FIG. 11

GFCI

GROUND LUG TOWARDS RECEPTACLE STRIP

MAKE ALL CONNECTIONS TO "LINE" SIDE OF GFCI.
WHITE WIRE TO "WHITE" SCREW
BLACK WIRE TO "HOT" SCREW
GREEN WIRE TO "GREEN" SCREW

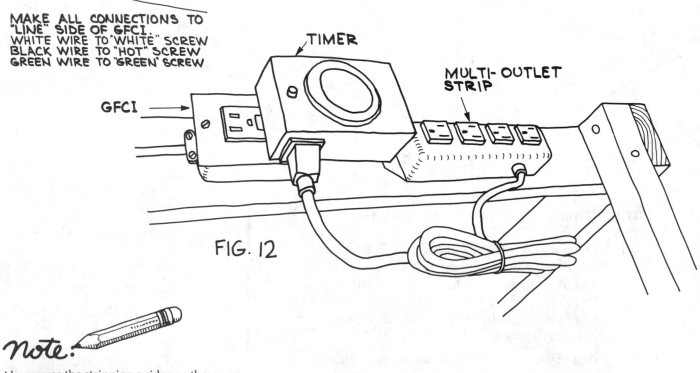

TIMER

MULTI-OUTLET STRIP

GFCI

FIG. 12

note!

Always use the stripping guides on the GFCI receptacles for stripping back to bare wire when attaching wire to the GFCI receptacle. Also, whenever stripping wire to be connected by wire nuts, be sure that no bare wire is exposed below the end of the wire nut.

Installing Lights

1. Wiring Light Fixtures

If you must add longer cords to your fixtures, repeat Steps 1 through 5 for each fixture.

Step 1.   Open up the light fixture by removing the retaining hardware or following manufacturer's directions. If there is an existing cord, follow where the existing cord enters the fixture until the inner wires terminate at wire nuts. Remove the wire nuts and the cord. Make a mental note of where all wires are connected.

Step 2.   Cut a 40" length of 16/3 cable and install a three-prong plug following same directions as in Wiring Power Supply, Steps 1 and 2 (see figure 9).

Step 3.   Remove from the opposite end of the cable, 4-6" of outer insulation and ½" of insulation from the ends of the three inner wires, as in Wiring Power Supply, Step 3.

Step 4.   Feed cable cord through hole in the end of fixture until wire ends meet ballast connections. Be sure to leave at least 1" of unstripped cable inserted into fixture. Place one Romex connector where the cable enters the fixture and secure it tightly as in figure 13.

Step 5.   Attach the new cord to the fixture, making sure to connect the new inner wires to the appropriate wires in the fixture, as shown in figure 13. Use wire nuts to make all connections. Reattach cover to light fixture.

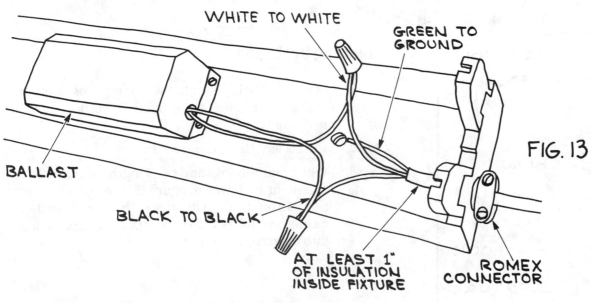

WHITE TO WHITE

GREEN TO GROUND

FIG. 13

BALLAST

BLACK TO BLACK

AT LEAST 1"
OF INSULATION
INSIDE FIXTURE

ROMEX CONNECTOR

OTHER WIRING OMITTED FOR CLARITY

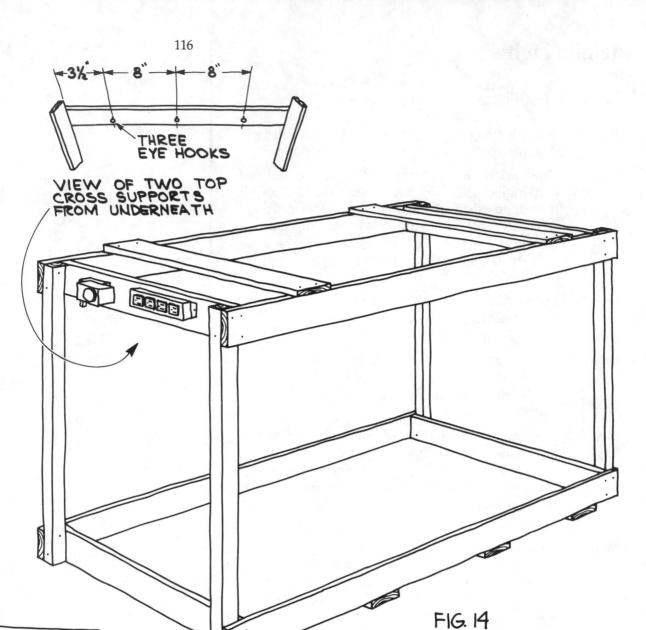

← 3½" → ← 8" → ← 8" →

THREE
EYE HOOKS

VIEW OF TWO TOP
CROSS SUPPORTS
FROM UNDERNEATH

FIG. 14

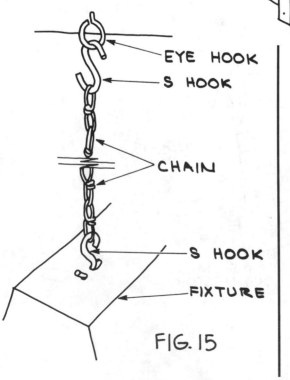

EYE HOOK

S HOOK

CHAIN

S HOOK

FIXTURE

FIG. 15

2. Mounting the Lights

Step 1. Screw six eye hooks into the two top cross supports of the wood frame, following the direction shown in figure 14.

Step 2. Cut six lengths of chain 36" long.

Step 3. Using four S-hooks and two lengths of chain, hang each light as shown in figure 15. Close the bottom S-hooks on the light fixtures with pliers. Install fluorescent tubes with tube guards. Plug each light into the receptacle strip.

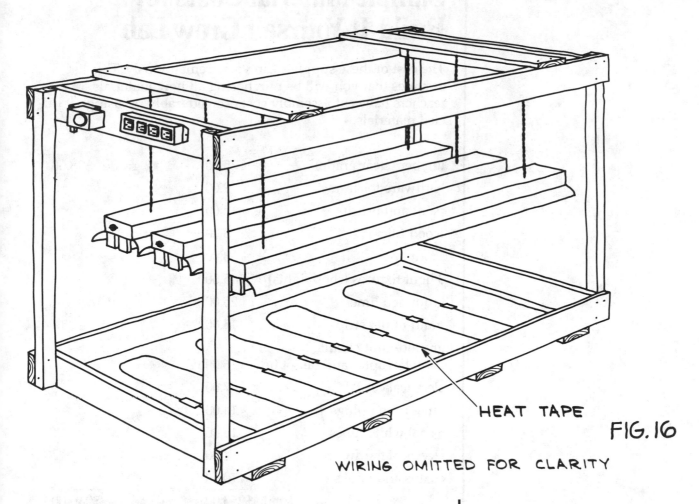

HEAT TAPE

FIG. 16

WIRING OMITTED FOR CLARITY

3. Installing a Heating Cable (Optional)

Step 1. If self-regulating cable is used, follow directions that come with heating cable for connecting the end cap and plug.

Step 2. Unless you have a plastic tray, lay a 28″ x 54″ plastic sheet in the base of the Grow Lab frame with edges at the same level as the top of the rails.

Step 3. Lay the heating cable over the plastic in the bottom of the unit, as illustrated in figure 16, making sure not to cross the cable back over itself.

Step 4. Tape cable in place using electrical or duct tape. (During operation, the cable will be covered with 2″ of moist sand/perlite, or with capillary matting.)

Step 5. Plug the heating cable directly into the ground fault receptacle. Do not plug heating cable into multi-outlet strip or timer as that will turn cable on and off.

Sample Material Costs for a Build-It-Yourself Grow Lab

The cost of these supplies can vary tremendously. This list assumes that you will be purchasing all new materials. Many teachers have cut assembly costs considerably by using recycled materials.

lumber (clear grade)	$75.00	#2 grade	$38.00
hardware for frame	9.00		
paint and brush	12.00		
wood filler	3.00		
sandpaper	3.00		
3 light fixtures (shop lights)	45.00		
grounded timer	25.00		
multi-outlet strip	15.00		
ground-fault circuit interrupter and outlet box	16.00		
electrical cord	7.00		
three-prong plugs	14.00		
6 cool white tubes	15.00		
electrical hardware	4.00		
chains and hooks	10.00		
Total:	$253.00		$216.00

Appendix E

Resources

Indoor Gardening Books

The Edible Indoor Garden. Peggy Hardigree. 1980. St. Martin's Press, New York, NY. 298 pages. Highly recommended for indoor gardeners. It offers a thorough explanation of basic plant needs, specific cultural requirements of many crops, and an extensive resource list.

Fun with Growing Herbs Indoors. George and Virginie Elbert. 1974. Crown Publishers, New York, NY. 192 pages. Nicely illustrated, practical guide to raising many types of herbs indoors.

Gardening Indoors Under Lights. Frederick H. and Jacqueline L. Kranz. 1971. Viking Press Inc., New York, NY 242 pages. A handy reference for information on different types of lighting, constructing an indoor garden, and basic techniques for growing under lights.

*Greenhouse Gardener's Companion. Shane Smith. 1992. Fulcrum Publishing, Golden, CO. 531 pages. Complete and easy to follow. Everything you need to know to grow food successfully in a greenhouse.

*Guide to School Greenhouses. 1995. National Gardening Association, Burlington, VT. 24 pages. A guide to providing good growing conditions, engaging students in exploring how greenhouses work, and integrating greenhouse projects into your curriculum.

The New Seed Starter's Handbook. Nancy Bubel. 1988. Rodale Press, Emmaus, PA. Contains a wealth of information on starting and saving seeds, and includes recipes for making your own growing mix. Also includes information on caring for seedlings in both natural and artificial light gardens.

Rodale's Encyclopedia of Indoor Gardening. Ann Halpin, Ed. 1980. Rodale Press, Emmaus, PA. 902 pages. A comprehensive guide to growing foliage plants, herbs, and some vegetables in the home or greenhouse. It includes basic techniques for raising plants indoors and an encyclopedia of more than 250 houseplants.

note.

Resources marked with an asterisk (*) are available from the National Gardening Association. Call (800) 538-7476 to request a catalog, or visit our web site at *http://catalog.garden.org*. Check your library or book stores for other titles.

Resource Books for Teachers

*Accessible Gardening for People with Physical Disabilities.
Janeen R. Adil. 1994. Woodbine House, Bethesda, MD. 300 pages. A practical and inspirational approach for gardeners of all ages who must overcome physical challenges. Includes plans for container gardens, sources for tools, and lists of appropriate plant varieties.

*Beyond the Bean Seed. Nancy A. Jurenka and Rosanne J. Blass. 1996. Teacher Ideas Press, Englewood, CO. 194 pages. A collection of ideas for connecting children's literature, language arts and creative activities with gardening and literacy.

Botany for All Ages: Discovering Nature Through Activities for Children and Adults. Jorie Hunken and The New England Wildflower Society. 1989, revised 1993. The Globe Pequot Press, Old Saybrook, CT. 184 pages. Information and activities organized around the principles of observation, experimentation, and self-expression. Activities are specific and informative, yet open-ended to allow for spontaneity of learning.

*Bottle Biology. Bottle Biology Project, University of Wisconsin-Madison. 1993. Kendall/Hunt Publishing Co., Dubuque, IA. 127 pages. Filled with ideas for using plastic bottles and other recyclable materials to teach about science and the environment, including activities with compost columns, spider habitats, and slime molds.

*Digging Deeper: Integrating Youth Gardens into Schools and Communities. Joseph Kiefer and Martin Kemple. 1998. Common Roots Press, Montpelier, VT. 146 pages. A how-to-guide designed for teachers, parents, and community workers who are interested in creating children's gardens that are linked to community heritage and food security. Includes photos, case studies, curriculum activities, and sample garden designs.

*Eco-Inquiry: A Guide to Ecological Learning Experiences for the Upper Elementary/Middle Grades. Kathleen Hogan, Institute of Ecosystem Studies. 1994. Kendall/Hunt Publishing Co., Dubuque, IA. 392 pages. A "whole science" curriculum embedding inquiry-based, investigative science within multidisciplinary learning. Detailed, classroom-tested lesson plans, practical teaching strategies, assessment tips, and cross-curricular extensions.

*Exploring Classroom Hydroponics. 1995. National Gardening Association, Burlington, VT. 24 pages. The basics of hydroponic growing; includes information on how to set up classroom systems, as well as activities to engage students' hands and minds.

*Exploring with Wisconsin Fast Plants. Paul Williams, University of Wisconsin-Madison. 1995. Kendall/Hunt Publishing Co., Dubuque, IA. 288 pages. Details how to use Wisconsin Fast Plants, which can grow from seed to seed in the classroom in just 40 days, to inspire student investigations of plant growth, life cycles, environmental issues, and heredity. Includes illustrated growing instructions, stories, learning games, and student worksheets.

Gardening for Maximum Nutrition. Jerry Minnich. 1983. Rodale Press, Emmaus, PA. 220 pages. Discusses varieties of vegetables and fruits that are high in nutrients. Provides information on harvest, storage, and preservation practices that maintain maximum nutritional value.

*The Growing Classroom. Life Lab Science Program. 1990. Addison-Wesley Publishing, Menlo Park, CA. 480 pages. A teacher's manual (grades 2-6) featuring strategies for managing garden-based science instruction. Includes information on planning a garden laboratory, facilitating investigative lessons on ecology and nutrition, and involving the community.

Growing with Gardening. Bibby Moore. 1987. Revised 1989. University of North Carolina Press, Chapel Hill, NC. 244 pages. A guidebook for health professionals, teachers, and rehabilitation specialists that offers ideas for teaching people with special needs about gardening. It outlines a program of weekly plant activities, featuring more than 250 activity ideas.

*GrowLab: Activities for Growing Minds. Eve Pranis and Joy Cohen. 1990. National Gardening Association, Burlington, VT. 307 pages. A K-8 curriculum guide to help you spark students' curiosity about plants and engage them in thinking and acting like scientists. Covers key concepts such as basic needs, reproduction, diversity, adaptations, and interdependence.

*In the Three Sisters Garden: Native American Stories and Seasonal Activities for the Curious Child. JoAnne Dennee. 1995. Common Roots Press, Montpelier, VT. 373 pages. Stories and activities centered around Native American corn, bean, and squash gardens; includes gardening and cooking methods as well as Native American arts and traditions.

Let's Grow! Linda Tilgner. 1988. Storey Communications, Inc., Pownal, VT. 208 pages. Written for parents, youth group leaders, and teachers; features 72 different garden adventures ranging from planting and raising an outdoor patchwork salad quilt to creating desert dish gardens.

Looking at Plants. David Suzuki. 1985. Revised 1992. John Wiley & Sons, New York, NY. 96 pages. An activity book to help kids and adults explore the exciting world of plants. Illustrated activities contain concise step-by-step instructions for each plant project.

*National Gardening Association Gardening Guides. Revised 1995. National Gardening Association, Burlington, VT. Nine books, available individually or as a set. Each book is a guide to growing, harvesting, preserving, and cooking vegetables. Series includes: Potatoes; Beans; Onions; Cauliflower, Broccoli & Cabbage; Peas & Peanuts; Cucumbers, Melons & Squash; Corn; Eggplant, Okra & Peppers; Root Crops..

National Gardening Association Guide to Kids' Gardening. Lynn Ocone and Eve Pranis. 1983, revised 1987. National Gardening Association, Burlington, VT. 148 pages. A comprehensive how-to guide for teachers, youth leaders, and parents. Thoroughly covers topics such as planning and organizing a garden program, designing and maintaining a site, and raising money. The book also highlights many successful projects from around the country, and describes more than 70 creative and educational gardening activities.

note:

Incorporate gardening into your curriculum with National Gardening Association's companion book, **GrowLab: Activities for Growing Minds.**

Plants Improving Our Environment. Soil and Water Conservation Society, 7515 Northeast Ankeny Road, Ankeny, IA 50021; (800) 843-7645. 16 pages. Pamphlet explains how plants improve environmental quality by guarding against erosion absorbing pollutants, and reducing noise. Do-it-yourself projects help children to understand plant functions.

*Project Seasons: Hands-on Activities for Discovering the Wonders of the World. Deborah Parella. 1995. Shelburne Farms, Shelburne, VT. 318 pages. A collection of hands-on activities and teaching ideas for elementary educators that uses the school-year seasons of fall, winter, and spring to integrate science, agriculture, and environmental themes into the curriculum.

Resource Guide to Educational Materials About Agriculture: A Project of Agriculture in the Classroom. U.S. Department of Agriculture, 1996. Agriculture in the Classroom, USDA, Room 3534-South, 1400 Independence Ave., Washington, DC 20250; (202) 720-7925. 68 pages. A thorough listing of materials and curriculum guides that teach about agriculture and related issues, such as agricultural history, technology, economics, policy issues, and careers. Also available on their web site at: *www.reeusda.gov/serd/hep/agclass.htm*

Seeds of Change: The Story of Cultural Exchange after 1492. Sharryl Davis Hawke and James E. Davis. 1992. Addison-Wesley Publishing Co., Menlo Park, CA. 94 pages. A fascinating series exploring the richness resulting from the cultural encounters between the Old and New Worlds since 1492, including how plants such as corn, potatoes, and sugarcane forever changed life here and abroad. Series includes text and grade-level workbooks, *Discovering Seeds of Change*.

*Sowing the Seeds of Success: How to Start and Sustain a Kids' Gardening Project in Your Community. Marcia Eames-Sheavly. 1999. National Gardening Association, Burlington, VT. 32 pages. Defines the organizational steps needed to initiate a gardening project that involves kids and the community, and to ensure program success over the long term.

Sunflower Houses: Garden Discoveries for Children of All Ages. Sharon Lovejoy. 1991, reissued 1995. Interweave Press, Inc., Loveland, CO. 144 pages. Garden stories, poems, activities, and projects that inspire curiosity and lasting memories.

*Terrarium Habitats. Kimi Hosourne. 1994. Lawrence Hall of Science, Berkeley, CA. 84 pages. Helps students design, construct, and explore life in classroom terrariums, helping to deepen student understanding of the connection of all living things.

*The Victory Garden Kid's Book. Marjorie Waters. 1988, revised 1994. The Globe Pequot Press, Old Saybrook, CT. 148 pages. A colorful guide to gardening with children. Step-by step instructions for each aspect of gardening, from digging in the spring, to harvesting in the fall, to making compost.

*The Wonderful World of Wigglers. Julia Hand. 1995. Common Roots Press, Montpelier, VT. 164 pages. A cross-disciplinary guide that encourages children to explore the connection between earthworms, the health of the soil, growing food, and sustainability. Includes many inquiry-based activities and projects using earthworms in the classroom.

*Worms Eat My Garbage. Mary Applehof. 1982, revised 1997. Flower Press, Kalamazoo, MI. 162 pages. A thorough guide to setting up and maintaining a worm composting system, inviting explorations of recycling concepts in the classroom by observing how worms compost food waste.

Books for Young Gardeners

Bean and Plant. Christine Back and Barrie Watts. 1984. Silver Burdett Co., Morristown, NJ. (Grades 1-4.) Contains a sequence of magnificent close-up photographs and simple text that follow a bean from seed to fruit to seed.

Being a Plant. Laurence Pringle. 1983. Thomas Y. Crowell Publishing, New York, NY. (Grades 6-8.) Explains the structure, reproduction, and photosynthesis of plants, and discusses the relationships between flowering plants, insects, and birds.

Blue Potatoes, Orange Tomatoes. Rosalind Creasy. 1994. Sierra Club, San Francisco, CA. Everything you need to know to grow a garden full of fruits and vegetables in unexpected colors. Detailed instructions for growing eight different "rainbow crops," including recipes for the harvest.

Eddie's Green Thumb. Carolyn Haywood. 1980. William Morrow and Co., New York, NY. (Grades 3-7.) The story of a boy and his classmates learning about gardening when they begin a Green Thumb project.

From Flower to Fruit. Anne Ophelia Dowden. 1984. Thomas Y. Crowell Publishing Co., New York, NY. (Grades 5-6.) Contains clear explanations and illustrations that explain fertilization, seed production, and maturation of various fruits.

*Garden Crafts for Kids. Diane Rhoades. 1995. Sterling Publishing Co., New York, NY. Fifty garden craft projects that encourage exploration, invention, and imagination; and creative ideas for designing gardens. Great for group and family projects.

*Gardening Wizardry for Kids. L. Patricia Kite. 1995. Barron's Educational Series, Inc., Hauppauge, NY. A colorful, kid-friendly book containing histories and folklore of common fruits, vegetables, and herbs. Includes indoor growing projects and fascinating investigations.

Gardens from Garbage: How to Grow Indoor Plants from Recycled Kitchen Scraps. Judith E. Handelsman. 1993. The Millbrook Press, Brookfield, CT. Ideas and instructions for starting plants from seeds and plant parts found in the kitchen.

The Great Seed Mystery for Kids. Peggy Henry. 1992. Avon Books, New York, NY. (Grades K & up.) Explores and investigates the world of seeds, including types of seeds, where they come from, what seeds need to grow, and more. Many indoor and outdoor activities.

The Hidden Magic of Seeds. Dorothy Shuttlesworth. 1976. Rodale Press, Emmaus, PA. (Grades 3-6.) Describes seed formation, growth, transport, and various uses. Also contains some activities for investigating seeds.

How Seeds Travel. Cynthia Overbeck. 1982. Lerner Publishing Co., Minneapolis, MN. (Grades 3-6.) A children's science book that describes how seeds travel by wind, water, and on people and animals.

The Reason for a Flower. Ruth Heller. 1983. Grosset & Dunlap, New York, NY. (Grades K-4.) A beautifully illustrated book covering flower formation, pollination, and variations.

The Rose in My Garden. Arnold and Anita Lobel. 1984. William Morrow & Company, New York, NY. (Grades K-4.) Lovely illustrations complement a sequential story about the plants and animals that dwell in a garden.

This Year's Garden. Cynthia Rylant. 1984, reprinted 1987. Aladdin Books, New York, NY. (Grades K-3.) A beautifully illustrated children's book that tells the story of a garden, from spring planting through preserving the harvest.

The Tiny Seed. Eric Carle. 1987. Picture Book Studio, Natick, MA. (Grades K-3.) Colorful illustrations and an exciting text tell the story of the life cycle of a flower through the dramatic adventures of a tiny seed.

Audiovisual Materials

Get Ready, Get Set, Grow. 15-minute video. 1988. Brooklyn Botanic Garden, 1000 Washington Avenue, Brooklyn, NY 11225. Introduces children to the wonder of plant growth and the basics of gardening. Includes two booklets: *A Kid's Guide to Good Gardening* and *Ideas for Parents and Teachers*.

*GrowLab: A Growing Experience. 14-minute introductory video. 1991. National Gardening Association, Burlington, VT. Students creatively share their thoughts on learning science with GrowLab and "state the case" for hands-on, garden-based instruction.

*Indoor Gardening: Advice from GrowLab Classrooms. 35-minute video. 1991. National Gardening Association, Burlington, VT. This video guides you through the basics of successful indoor classroom gardening, from transplanting tomatoes to making cuttings. Experienced classroom gardening teachers demonstrate how to engage students in everything from planting to pollinating cucumbers.

*Plant a Question: Using the GrowLab Teaching Cycle. 30-minute video. 1991. National Gardening Association, Burlington, VT. Using actual GrowLab classroom footage, this video portrays how to use the GrowLab teaching cycle as a framework for engaging science lessons. You'll see teachers using a variety of strategies — concept maps, brainstorming, controlled experiments — to guide student-centered explorations.

Indoor Gardening Equipment Suppliers

Many supplies can be purchased locally. National Gardening Association offers many indoor gardening supplies, including several GrowLab Indoor Garden models, pots, labels, potting mix, fertilizer, seed collections, wide-spectrum flourescent tubes and fixtures,

Perma-Nest trays, moisture grids, capillary matting, and timers. Also available from NGA's *Gardening with Kids!* catalog are curriculum resources for indoor and outdoor gardening, outdoor gardening equipment, greenhouses, worm composting supplies, and hydroponics units to expand your gardening curriculum.

National Gardening Association
180 Flynn Avenue
Burlington, VT 05401
(800) 538-7476
http://catalog.garden.org

Seed Suppliers

There are many mail-order seed companies. The following list includes just a sampling of companies you can contact for seed catalogs. Many catalogs also include growing information as well as pots, fertilizers, and other supplies.

W. Atlee Burpee & Company
300 Park Avenue
Warminster, PA 18974
(800) 333-5808
www.burpee.com

Ferry-Morse Seeds
PO Box 1620
Fulton, KY 42041
(800) 283-6400
www.ferry-morse.com

Johnny's Selected Seeds
Foss Hill Road
Albion, ME 04910
(207) 437-4301
www.johnnyseeds.com

Park Seed Company
1 Parkton Ave
Greenwood, SC 29647
(800) 845-3369
www.parkseed.com

Shepherd's Garden Seeds
30 Irene Street
Torrington, CT 06790
(860) 482-3638
www.shepherdseeds.com

Territorial Seed Company
PO Box 157
Cottage Grove, OR 97424
(541) 942-9547
www.territorial-seed.com

Organizational Resources

There are many national horticultural organizations with state and local chapters or affiliates. Members of these local chapters may be interested in sponsoring classroom gardening programs or in providing technical assistance and advice to indoor gardening classrooms. For information on such groups in your area, contact the following national headquarters:

Agriculture in the Classroom
U.S. Department of Agriculture
Room 3534-South
1400 Independence Avenue
Washington, DC 20250
(202) 720-7925
www.reeusda.gov/serd/hep/agclass.htm

American Association of Botanical Gardens and Arboreta
351 Longwood Road
Kennett Square, PA 19348
(610) 925-2500
www.aabga.org

American Community Gardening Association
100 N 20th Street 5th Floor
Philadelphia, PA 19103
(215) 988-8845
www.communitygarden.org

American Horticultural Therapy Association
909 York Street
Denver, CO 80206
(301) 948-3010
www.ahta.org

Gardeners of America
5560 Merle Hay Road
Johnston, 1A 50131
(515) 278-0295

National 4-H Council
7100 Connecticut Avenue
Chevy Chase, MD 20815
(301) 961-2840

National Council of State Garden Clubs
4401 Magnolia Avenue
St. Louis, MO 63110
(314) 776-7574
www.gardenclub.org

Future Farmers of America
6060 FFA Drive, PO Box 68960
Indianapolis, IN 46268
(317) 802-6060

The National Gardening Association

The National Gardening Association (NGA) is a nonprofit organization established in 1972. Our mission is to sustain the essential values of life and community, renewing the fundamental links between people, plants, and the Earth. Through gardening, the organization promotes environmental responsibility, advances multidisciplinary learning and scientific literacy, and creates partnerships that restore and enhance communities. The NGA disseminates information in a variety of forms (magazine, books, radio) to promote gardening as a learning tool, a science, and an art.

Our education division implements programs using plants and gardens as contexts to teach students to become active inquirers and problem solvers and to foster in them the value of caring responsibly for the environment.

Gardening with Kids! Catalog. Features exemplary educational materials for using plants and gardens as living learning laboratories. Includes indoor and outdoor gardening equipment, curricular, and thematic resources such as books on butterfly gardening, composting with worms, Native American gardens, and more.

Growing Ideas: A Journal of Garden-Based Learning. Published three times a year, this 12-page newsletter features thematic articles covering topics from butterfly gardens to school compost projects. It reports how teachers use plants to spark science learning, and highlights free resources and grant opportunities.

Kids and Classrooms Web Site. Includes information about educational programs and grants, Growing Ideas articles, an online Teaching Tools catalog, and direct links to e-mail pals from other growing classrooms. Also featured are links to other plant- and garden-based sites.

GrowLab K-8 Science Program. NGA's National Science Foundation-funded GrowLab program includes indoor garden laboratories, curriculum materials that align with the National Science Education Standards, a national network of trained consultants, and professional development training manuals and videos. GrowLab's inquiry-based teaching approach helps students learn to think and act like scientists, as they use their own questions and observations as springboards for learning.

Youth Garden Grants Program. Every year, each of 300 schools and youth groups are awarded an assortment of tools, seeds, and garden products valued at more than $750 to help initiate or sustain a gardening program. Applications are available in March for a November 1 deadline.

National Gardening magazine. Our bimonthly magazine for gardening enthusiasts contains the latest information on growing fruits, vegetables, roses and other ornamental plants, plus contact information for seed, equipment, and other companies in the gardening industry.

For more information about our materials and programs, contact:

National Gardening Association
180 Flynn Avenue, Burlington, Vermont 05401
Phone: (800) 538-7476 • FAX: (802) 863-5962
E-mail: eddept@garden.org
www.garden.org/edu

Index